ACCOUNT PLANNING GROUP

2001 Creative Planning Awards

apg

A publication of the
Account Planning Group
16 Creighton Avenue
London N10 1NU
Telephone: +44 (0) 20 8444 3692
Facsimile: +44 (0) 20 8883 9953
E-mail: mail@apg.org.uk
Website: http://www.apg.org.uk

Contact: Steve Martin

Editors
Peter Dann
& Marie-Louise Neill

Printed in England by
CB Printing Services
Dartmouth, Devon

©Account Planning Group

ISBN NO: 0-9525237-4-4

Contents

Foreword

This book records the fifth occasion that the APG has conducted the Creative Planning Awards, our biennial celebration of the best that account planning can offer. These Awards have now become a significant and established fixture, and remain the only awards competition to recognise, encourage and reward upstream thinking in marketing communications.

In the lifetime of the Awards, the world of account planning and communications in general has changed enormously. While agencies and client companies alike have embraced the discipline of planning, the role of the account planner has expanded to cover planning in an array of different media and across an ever-widening range of types of brands. In all this, the link between creative planning and great creative work is as critical as ever.

We overhauled our categories for submissions in 2001 to encourage entries into every category that describe the contribution of account planning to any campaign in any media. Rather than separating broadcast, print and 'below-the-line' we designed categories that we hoped take account of the different contributions planning makes to new and existing campaigns in different markets, regardless of the media employed by the eventual executions. As a result campaigns were judged against others with similar objectives rather than with similar executions.

We also expanded the area of these awards for specific craft skills. Although these could be awarded to any paper, whether shortlisted or not, this year these awards tended to go to those which also won in their category. Consequently, in this book we have grouped the craft skill awards within these categories.

2001's entry is remarkable for what it says about the health of planning, and how it has matured in the eight years since the Awards began. The papers in this book come from a very broad range of backgrounds: different sizes and types of agency, different market sectors, media and budgets, different marketing issues to address, and perhaps most importantly, the widest ever range of types of planning and types of planner.

One thing unites them, however, and that is the quality of the thinking. Every paper included in this book is a fine example of how good, thoughtful planning has led to better, more creative advertising, and every author should be proud of their contribution not just to their own client's campaign but now to the discipline of planning in general. In this company, being shortlisted is an achievement.

A pleasant side effect of this depth of quality is that choosing winners was harder than ever. Our thanks should go more than ever to the panel of judges, who volunteered for what turned out to be a demanding if rewarding task.

Finally, but perhaps most importantly, one last opportunity to thank our sponsors. It is a fact rather than a figure of speech that these Awards could not happen without them.

Peter Dann, *APG Vice-Chair*

Rules, Categories and Prizes

The submissions that win APG Creative Planning Awards are those that best demonstrate how account planning made a difference to the creative work. It is the link between innovative thinking and excellent creative work that is rewarded. The jury evaluates the original insight; how that insight manifested itself in the creative brief or briefing; and how well the creative team was able to utilise that insight. All entries are for communications appearing within the last two years and a submission to any category can represent work in any media. The author (or at least one of the authors in the case of a joint entry) must be an APG member. Papers are shortlisted on the basis of a 2000-word written paper and prizes are awarded following a 30-minute presentation to the final jury. There are two types of prize: Category Awards and Special Prizes.

Categories:

Campaigns for established service brands
A campaign in any media for an existing and marketed service brand

Campaigns for established product brands
A campaign in any media for an existing and marketed product

New brands or new advertisers
A campaign in any media that either launches a new brand or represents its first piece of marketing activity

Multi-market campaigns
A campaign in any media, specifically planned to run in more than one country including the UK

Public Service & Charity
A campaign designed to influence a segment of the public to donate to charity or to change attitudes or behaviour on an issue of public concern

Innovative approaches to marketing communications
A campaign in any media, involving a particularly original and innovative approach to communication at any stage of the campaign's development

Special Prizes
- Best consumer insight
- Best strategic insight
- Best creative brief and briefing
- Best contribution to media thinking
- Most innovative qualitative research design
- Best use of research

All papers entered, not just those shortlisted for a category award, are eligible for a special prize. The last two special prizes are granted by the shortlisting panel and the remainder are decided jointly by the shortlisting panel and the final jury.

Grand Prix
The Grand Prix is awarded for the best overall submission drawn from the gold winners in the six main categories.

Acknowledgements

The Account Planning Group would like to thank the advertising agencies, category and special prize sponsors and individuals who made the fifth APG Creative Planning Awards an outstanding success.

Category & Special Prize Sponsors
2cv:research
Denise Williams Executive
     Recruitment
Express Train
Hall & Partners Europe
IPA
Leapfrog Research & Planning
Mellor Watts International
Millward Brown
NABS
The Nursery
The Research Business International
Red Spider
Wardle McLean Strategic Research
     Consultancy

Agency Sponsors
Abbott Mead Vickers BBDO
Euro RSCG Wnek Gosper
J Walter Thompson
Leo Burnett
Ogilvy
Publicis
Rainey Kelly Campbell Roalfe/Y&R
Saatchi & Saatchi
WCRS

Campaign Magazine
The Account Planning Group would like to acknowledge the continuing support of *Campaign* magazine

2001 Awards Jury

Shortlisting Panel

Christine Asbury, *APG Committee*
Vanella Jackson,
　　Abbott Mead Vickers BBDO
Max Burt,
　　Freelance Planning Consultant
Jane Cunningham, *Tribal DDB*
Richard Huntington,
　　HHCL & Partners
Alison Meredith, *Proximity London*
Hilde Oord, *J Walter Thompson*
Charlie Snow,
　　Delaney Lund Knox Warren

Jury

Janet Grimes *(APG Chair)*,
　　Planning Consultant
Peter Dann *(APG Vice-Chair)*,
　　The Nursery
John Bartle
Chris Green, *ICI Paints*
Leon Jaume, *WCRS*
Louise Jones, *PHD*
Dominic Mills, *Campaign*
Adam Morgan, *Eatbigfish*
Rory Sutherland,
　　Ogilvy One Worldwide

Awards Committee Members

Janet Grimes
Peter Dann
Christine Asbury
Vanella Jackson
Marie-Louise Neill

2001 Awards Jury

Left to right:
Leon Jaume, Dominic Mills, Janet Grimes,
John Bartle, Chris Green, Louise Jones,
Adam Morgan, Rory Sutherland, Peter Dann

Campaigns for established service brands

The APG Creative Planning Awards

Category Sponsor

denise williams
Executive Recruitment

In common with the APG Awards, I share the goal of spotting talented planners and developing the careers of those with the abilities to push boundaries and look at things in a new light. These planners help produce advertising that really does make a difference, builds brands and sells product. The APG Awards provide planners with the opportunity to demonstrate their creative thinking and be acknowledged for it. The winning entries provide younger planners with examples of planning excellence, help them to develop their skills and encourage them to enter future papers themselves. I am delighted to be a sponsor of great thinking.

Denise Williams Executive Recruitment
2 Naseby Close, London NW6 4EY Telephone: 020 7372 6300
denise@denisewilliams.co.uk

Grand Prix Sponsor

Leapfrog Research and Planning is proud to be associated with the APG awards as it acknowledges the combination of inspiration and perspiration that contributes to best practice in planning. Whilst the most enlightened agencies and thinkers in the industry recognise the contribution that planning and research can make to the development of distinctive advertising, planners are still easy targets for some who see them as the enemy of "creativity". These awards are in praise of the "art" that is good planning.

Leapfrog Research & Planning
First Floor, 13 High Street, Windsor SL4 1LD Telephone: 01753 833344
www.leapfrogresearch.co.uk

UN.NOTICE.CED

Last Thursday Scott Haynes one of our new dedicated Platform Assistants helped move a group of day-trippers obstructing an exit at Euston which helped the northbound platform clear which helped your train leave on time which helped you get to work on time all of which we hope you didn't notice.

NON.EVENT

Last week Ayisha Connolly the newest member of our Litter Collecting Team picked up a drinks can left on the northbound platform at Bank which meant it didn't roll onto the track which meant it didn't get trapped beneath a train which meant you didn't get delayed just thought you might like to know.

UN NEWS WORTHY

On Wednesday Gavin Holmes one of our new Customer Care Assistants at Oxford Circus showed a crowd of Belgian students the right way to the platform for Waterloo which meant they got the Eurostar on time which meant the station was clear for rush hour which meant you made your train and would never have known any different.

LONDON UNDERGROUND

GOLD & GRAND PRIX
Partners BDDH

Campaigns for established service brands
sponsor: Denise Williams Executive Recruitment
Grand Prix
sponsor: Leapfrog Research & Planning

Litter pickers make the Tube run faster

This paper demonstrates how careful thinking about developments seemingly unrelated to service was coupled with consumer insight to produce a compelling campaign. As a result, amid a very public climate of criticism and ill feeling, advertising was able to demonstrate how these apparently peripheral initiatives such as litter pickers could improve the things that matter to customers: reliability and punctuality.

Winner: Jane Lingham
Agency: Partners BDDH
Creative Director: Will Awdry
Art Directors: Matthew Anderson, Steve Nicholls
Copywriters: Matthew Anderson, Steve Nicholls
Typographer: Andy Breese
Client: Transport for London
Product: London Underground

The background

Making great ads for London Underground is tough. All of London and a great deal of the rest of Britain knows the Tube is far from a flawless product and that lack of investment is manifesting itself in operational problems throughout the entire network. It's now almost customary for the 'Good morning' greeting which accompanies a colleague's arrival in the office to be followed by "I've had an awful journey in this morning" and then subsequent tales of crammed tube carriages and train delays. Our biggest challenge therefore is that any perceptions we endeavour to change for the better can be undermined by experience of the service: in the run up to the launch of the campaign we are talking about, a significant section of the Victoria line had been shut for three weeks, news of an imminent reduction to the District line service had just broken[1], and escalators were causing disruption at a number of key stations (including Oxford Circus and Charing Cross).

The task

It was against this backdrop of negativity that we were asked to improve perceptions of the Underground among heavy users[2] by raising awareness of a number of changes taking place.

The improvements London Underground asked us to communicate were:

- More litter pickers.
- More CCTV cameras and more British Transport Police in stations.
- More station assistants and more customer help points.

'All positive changes and perfectly valid improvements in their own right' we thought, 'but quite small and perhaps a little contentious in the context of the bigger issues surrounding the Tube'. Delivering against our objective was going to be a very tough challenge.

The target

To add to our difficulties, heavy users were always going to be the hardest attitudinal audience to crack. This is because the majority are commuters who experience the Tube at its worst (during the morning and evening peaks when overcrowding is chronic). As a consequence they have the most negative brand perceptions, particularly when compared to those travelling out of rush hour, whose experience is much more positive.

It was therefore essential to target heavy users because:

1. They have the most negative perceptions of the Underground which meant we had more to gain by talking to them.

2. Personal opinion is a powerful tool in shaping overall brand perceptions and heavy users are one of the key drivers of negative word of mouth.

We also had to bear in mind that London Underground is a quasi-governmental organisation offering an essential service, and is therefore under public scrutiny from a number of key stakeholder parties (politicians, senior management, the Mayor's office, national Government, the media etc.). The *Evening Standard* had been quite negative about the Underground, running the headline, 'The Disgrace of London's Tube' the week before our campaign launched. Given that our heavy user target are three and a half times more likely to read it than the average Londoner, a prime consideration for any work we produced would be whether or not it could be used to fuel the ongoing public anti-Tube debate.

The expectation

This brief was not for the faint-hearted, and in such an adverse environment it's easy to question 'why advertise at all?'. The reason is that although these weren't enormous great changes which were going to revolutionise the Tube service, they were improvements nonetheless, and they were improvements that London Underground wanted to talk about.

We knew that public perception would not change overnight, but the intention was that over time all of these smaller changes would help contribute to a better Tube environment which would slowly help to chip away at some of the ingrained poor perceptions people held.

In terms of campaign effect, we were not expecting a revolutionary overhaul in perceptions of the Tube. The best outcome we could hope for was an incremental change in perceptions for the better. Bigger service changes still needed to take place, but everything has to start somewhere, and this was the first rung on a very long ladder.

We had our work cut out.

The bit that went wrong

As planners do, we began by writing a brief identifying what we believed were the key benefits to each of the improvements. They were:
- Litter pickers would mean a cleaner environment.
- More station assistants/help points would mean advice and help more to hand.
- More CCTV/British Transport Police would mean reduced crime on the Underground.

The creative team produced a series of concepts from the brief which all had a direct headline referring to the change being made. For example, with CCTV cameras – 'Now we can watch you read this poster about the improvements on the Underground', which we 'sense checked' with qualitative research among heavy Tube users.

19

The outcome

With hindsight, we can say that, perhaps a little unsurprisingly, the concepts completely bombed. Most thought that London Underground's intention to communicate the changes was little more than a joke given the much more important issues of overcrowding and an unreliable train service. The creative tone was considered too self-congratulatory and insensitive to Tube users (by light-heartedly involving Underground customers in the headline, the consensus of feeling was that London Underground were having a joke at their expense).

It seemed we could do nothing to make our target audience warm to our message because they were rejecting outright our changes as significant improvements. Moreover, because the topic of improvements on the Tube was such a sensitive one, talking about these minor changes began to fuel debates about the bigger problems, something we desperately needed to avoid. It was simply not deemed appropriate to be talking about more CCTV cameras given the ill-feeling surrounding the Tube at that time.

In response to the opposition we met from customers, we went back to try and re-define the problem. We still had to communicate the changes, but given the strength of negativity with which they were received, the question was how?

The insight

We thought carefully about what we had learned from research and concluded that if our target did not consider the improvements valuable enough to be worth talking about, this was because, in the context of the Underground's bigger problems, they weren't finding the benefits relevant enough to the issues that were top of mind. What we needed to do then was identify conclusively the real issues that bothered heavy users, and somehow find a way of linking our improvements to them. We went back over the previous 12 months brand research data and found they were rooted in the following areas:

● Reliability
● Safe service
● Frequent service
● Convenience
● Speed

It was during a conversation with the creative team that we noticed there was no mention of the peripheral issues surrounding the Tube at all, and instead these were all areas which had a direct impact on the actual running of the trains. Suddenly the penny dropped. People use the Tube to get from A to B, and as this was the most significant area in which the Tube was under-performing, of course this was what concerned our target. We had found our insight. What our users were really concerned about was their journeys.

The solution

With this in mind, we went back and looked harder at the potential benefits that the improvements offered. How could we possibly link cleaner stations to a more reliable service? Did the changes offer valuable improvements in less obvious ways than our first brief suggested? It seemed impossible. At least, it did until we started to look harder at the benefits we had already identified and what they could potentially mean to customers. We listed out all the changes being made and all the potential consequences of these changes and slowly a pattern emerged.

Although when we took the benefits at face value they offered a straightforward improvement, when we pushed our thinking a little further, we began to find ways in which they might impact on the service at a much more significant level.

We revised the potential benefits of each improvement:

● Litter pickers can prevent delays by stopping litter blowing onto tracks and jamming points.

● Customer care assistants can help trains leave on time by assisting customers to navigate their journey, thereby keeping platforms clear and reducing train dwell-time in stations.

● Help points can keep the service running smoothly by making sure journey interchanges are as quick as possible with immediate help and advice.

● British Transport Police can minimise disturbances by preventing crime, not just dealing with it once it has occurred.

● CCTV can prevent disruption to services by monitoring activity on the Underground, ensuring incidents are dealt with quickly and effectively.

By finding an insight into the real improvements the changes offered, and coupling this with an understanding about what really motivates our target audience, we were able to identify benefits which affect journeys, the main issue which concerned our target audience.

The creative work

The creative executions amplified this thought enormously using a format which mimicked traditional 'information' posters[3], the natural environment for communicating bad news. Whereas normally an information poster would have the headline 'Notice' or 'Incident' to catch people's attention, our headlines read 'unNoticed' and 'Incident didn't happen here'.

This was followed by a story highlighting a 'behind-the-scenes chain of events' which begins with one of our changes and results in an incident *not* happening, enabling the Tube to keep running smoothly. By using this type-only mock information format and flipping the outcome to a positive we made our message much more powerful.

Fictional names were used for staff (and customers where they appeared) which added warmth to the ads and helped customers see staff as individuals.

We researched the work qualitatively among eight paired depths and found the re-positioning of the improvements meant our heavy users now believed they were valid and worth talking about. In addition, the charm of the ads positioned the Tube favourably as a much friendlier, warmer environment.

But probably the most gratifying thing about the executions was their engaging, almost self-deprecating tone of voice which ensured there was no danger of overclaim about the improvements.

The results

The success we witnessed in research was reflected in the tracking results. At the peak of the campaign, awareness was at 73%, one of the highest scores London Underground has ever achieved for a poster campaign. We also achieved our much hoped for increase in favourable perceptions among those who had seen the campaign, and it seemed we had overcome the issue of irrelevance, with 64% of those who recalled the campaign believing it to be very or quite relevant to them.

Additionally, although the impact of our campaign on the London media and key opinion formers was harder to measure, there was no denunciation of the Tube's efforts within the London press, and we are aware of no politician using the improvements to exemplify 'the misguided direction of London Underground' for political gain.

The conclusion

This paper has demonstrated how a thorough understanding of our target audience and careful consideration of the benefits offered by specific service improvements, led to the production of a campaign which was relevant (64%), had strong cut through (73% awareness), and was persuasive.

Without the planning contribution outlined in this paper, it is likely we would have focussed our campaign on benefits which turned out to be neither relevant nor motivating to our target audience. Instead we were able to produce award winning and effective work which changed perceptions among London Underground's hardest attitudinal target.

[1] 'Tube Line Faces Massive Disruption', Dick Murray, *Evening Standard*, 15 September, 2000
[2] Heavy users are defined using TGI data as those who use the Tube five times or more per week
[3] The campaign ran on cross tracks (on the Underground), Double Royals (TfL's own on-system media space) and in press.

"My name is Kopi. When I first arrived here, I had to learn about everything."

"I learnt by asking questions."

'WHO WANTS TO BE A MILLIONAIRE?'

"They've taken questions and really made them work ... no darts, no Bully, no caravan."

"I should have stuck to questions, instead I had a Euro quiz."

SILVER
D'Arcy

Campaigns for established service brands
sponsor: Denise Williams Executive Recruitment

'When is a question better than an answer?'

While people wanted the sort of customer-oriented service Alliance + Leicester were about to offer, they were also deeply cynical about advertising for other banks that conveyed similar messages. Planning identified that offering questions when everyone else was claiming to offer answers, was a more powerful way of illustrating customer focus.

Winner: Robert Tansey
Agency: D'Arcy
Creative Director: Nick Hastings
Art Directors: Steve Drysdale, Paul Jordan, Angus Macadam
Copywriters: Steve Boswell, Paul Jordan, Angus Macadam
Client: Alliance + Leicester
Product: Alliance + Leicester brand campaign

A change in marketing focus

Since they'd demutualised in 1997 and become a bank, Alliance + Leicester's main business priority had been to recruit as many new customers as possible. This required a reliance on direct sales messages, the proliferation of which was now beginning to harm the brand. As a consequence, consideration among both customers and non-customers was falling.

A+L needed to reverse this trend by returning to a business model that redressed the balance between brand building and direct selling. What this required was brand-focussed advertising that would predispose consumers towards A+L before they started looking at different rates and products.

The brand vision

In order to survive in the ever more competitive world of financial services, A+L decided that it needed to become the most customer-focussed financial service provider, bar none. Only by treating people well and providing the right products for them as individuals could they ensure a growing loyal customer base that would, in turn, push shareholder value up to a level that protected A+L against potential hostile takeover bids.

Unfortunately, customer service is what a lot of other banks are trying to offer, because they all seem to have recognised 'en masse' that the balance of power has shifted towards the consumer. Banks are service providers, after all, and, if they don't provide good service, consumers are increasingly likely to vote with their feet.

Naturally we wanted to go and find out what consumers thought of other banks' attempts to give them good customer service, whether these were working, and if there was room for a different strategy to meet the same vision.

An opportunity and a challenge

We found out two very important things: first, that consumers do, indeed, want better, more personal service, so there was a need for the sort of brand vision A+L was proposing; second and more importantly, that any bank's claim of giving excellent service, of putting the customer first, is met with either gross cynicism or outright derision. Consumers have felt exploited for so long and felt so badly treated over so many years that any sort of overt customer service claim just isn't believed. After all, if the school bully suddenly comes over all nice and friendly and says he wants to be your best friend, do you take him at his word?

This means that no-one believes banks when they promise that they want to do what's right for their customers, resulting in a cynicism that was going to be extremely hard for us to break down. It was almost as if a brand proposition that went straight to customer service was too big a leap, that it stretched credibility beyond breaking point.

What we would have to do was give consumers a reason to believe that A+L were going to give them better service. We were going to have to show them how good customer service worked.

Towards a brand proposition

You might think that good customer service is just about giving people what they want, but it's not so straightforward in financial services. As a low interest, confusing category, people don't always know what they want. Customer service in a bank is nothing like customer service in a sandwich shop. It's not just a question of making sure you've got the right amount of choice and that your product is fresh and well put together (although, as a retailer, this is clearly part of it). Customer service in a bank is more like customer service in a doctor's surgery. First of all you've got to understand what's wrong and what's needed before you can start putting things right. And we found in our research that this was the basis of most consumers' frustration with banks: they make no effort to understand people or what they need.

In fact, understanding your customers is the basis of all good service. The better you understand them, the more you can help them.

Unfortunately, as a bank, claiming that you understand your customers is as flimsy and unbelievable as promising good customer service. To make people believe that you understand them, you have to show them how you're going to do it or they'll just dismiss you. So what we had to do was to drill down one stage further and find out how good understanding comes about. Consequently, we talked to people from different professions who relied on understanding as a key part of their job (a psychotherapist, a counsellor, a doctor and even a good old qualitative researcher) to find out how they went about gaining this understanding.

The pivotal moment

Here we made a key discovery. Although there were nuances in the type of understanding they were trying to reach, they all followed the same basic modus operandi: they asked questions. For each of them, questions were the principal tool by which they came to understand the problems, issues or points of view of the people they were dealing with.

They also said that part of the reason questions were such a good tool for doing this was that they set up the dynamics of an equal relationship when asked in the right way. Questions that truly seek to understand someone involve them in the process. The very fact of asking someone a question creates a dialogue, a reciprocal relationship and means that a certain trust is established. It means that a view is being sought, that someone is interested in them and that their response matters.

And this sign of interest is absolutely true in our social lives as well. If you were meeting someone for the first time, at a dinner party for example, and they didn't ask you many questions it would be a clear sign that they weren't really interested in you.

It therefore struck us that, in questions, in their power to generate understanding, we had the concrete building blocks we needed to get sceptical consumers to believe A+L's customer-focussed promise. By showing them how questions were going to help us to understand them and to serve them better, our promise would have real substance in comparison with the vacuous claims of other organisations. In questions we would have a powerful, distinctive and motivating communications tool – and one that, in total opposition to traditional banking relationships, treated them in an adult-to-adult fashion rather than like a naughty schoolboy.

The creative brief and briefing

The creatives weren't exactly as excited as we were about the brief ('to show how asking questions helps A+L understand their consumers and give them better service'). Their problem was that they personally found questions intrusive and thought it a dangerous strategy. And the fact is that questions can be intrusive, especially if they come from someone you don't properly trust, like a bank. Naturally we'd had these discussions among ourselves and, with the creative director's backing, had researched the strategy with consumers before briefing the teams. This provided us with evidence to overcome their anticipated cynicism.

The results showed that, when questions are presented in the way we intended, consumers actively embrace them as a positive thing: 'Alliance + Leicester want to understand exactly what you want. Questions imply understanding - in the long run, hopefully they'll get what each customer wants.' [1]

The briefing successfully persuaded the teams that we had a strategy that was both distinctive and motivating and then challenged them to develop work that showed questions in this positive, non-threatening way.

The creative execution

The creative leap actually came from our descriptions of how the professions we'd thought about all relied on questions to generate understanding. What the team saw from the consistency of the approaches to understanding was that it's not just professionals who rely on questions, but that we all do, whenever we encounter any unfamiliar situation. Questions are, in effect, the tool we constantly use to navigate our way round things we don't understand.

So they created the character of an eskimo, Kopi, who enabled the creatives to highlight this everyday reliance on questions without resorting to the cliché of inquisitive children and without patronising adults. He is a likeable, resourceful outsider, thrust into a totally alien environment and who succeeds in understanding and being understood by asking and being asked questions. In this way, he is able to get what is right for him.

His affinity with A+L comes from the fact that they, too, realise the importance of questions for understanding and helping people. Yet this not only helps them to understand their customers and their needs, but also helps them to get what's right for them in all areas relating to finance. In the second commercial, for example, Kopi is able to buy a better car because the questions A+L have supplied through their buyers' guides prevent a dodgy salesman from taking advantage of him.

Influencing the media choice

The media strategy had always intended to give extra saliency to the campaign through placing the ads in programming related to questions, such as quiz shows and current affairs forums. But we also had an early chance to demonstrate how the questions territory offered up creative media opportunities, when we noticed that sponsors of *Who Wants to be a Millionaire?* had decided not to renew their deal. In taking up the sponsorship we had the perfect, high profile media vehicle that could begin to associate Alliance + Leicester with questions.

Effectively running as a teaser campaign, the idents play off the bitterness of 70s game show hosts who tried to fill their show with gimmicks, while *Millionaire* has achieved much greater success by concentrating purely on the questions. As at A+L, questions are the answer. For the first time, the biggest TV phenomenon of recent years had a sponsor whose communications strategy sat perfectly alongside the content of the show, rather than using the borrowed interest of Chris Tarrant's catchphrases.

Results

Well, as *The Times*[2] put it, 'This [launch] advert is a rare beast in that it is genuinely amusing. But the humour makes a serious point: most people are lost and confused by the bewildering complexities of personal finance… but Alliance + Leicester [uses] questions to help it to understand its customers.'

This comment has been borne out by the tracking study [3] run to monitor the Alliance + Leicester brand and its advertising, with respondents rating A+L as 'using questions as a tool for understanding people' higher than any other bank. Consumers genuinely understand the beneficial nature of questions and appreciate their use in delivering good customer service. They believe in what the advertising has to offer, proving that Alliance + Leicester's questions are better than many other banks' supposed answers.

And, within Alliance + Leicester itself, two things give us great satisfaction about our strategy: the relevant use of questions now forms the basis of their entire customer service vision from advertising right through to staff training; and the share price has recovered to near record levels.

So, any questions?

[1] Cronk Dromgoole, strategic development research, October 2000
[2] *The Times*, 7 July, 2001
[3] HPI research group

TV:

"This is the magical rapport you get, banking with First Direct."

SILVER
WCRS

Campaigns for established service brands
sponsor: Denise Williams Executive Recruitment

From persuasion to mobilisation

First Direct has always targeted customers of rival banks. However, planning identified that this advertising approach was seen by current customers as unrepresentative of their bank, with the result that recommendation levels were falling. The new campaign aimed to mobilise recommendation by demonstrating the rapport between First Direct and its customers.

Winner: Dan Izbicki
Agency: WCRS
Creative Director: Leon Jaume
Art Director: Andy Dibb
Copywriter: Steve Little
Client: First Direct
Product: First Direct

Background

Being a First Direct customer is brilliant. If you don't believe me just go and ask one. In case there isn't a suitable candidate to hand, this is the sort of thing they are likely to say: "I think First Direct banking is the most efficient, friendly and extremcly helpful banking service I have ever used." (Customer e-mail, February 2001). Or "The best thing about them is that they don't act like a bank. Dealing with them feels very personal." (Focus group, November 2000).

In the dire and detested world of financial services, this is a bank that is utterly unique; its customers can't stop singing its praises.

If, like most of the population, you don't keep your hard-earned cash with First Direct, I suspect the views you hold of your bank are somewhat different. They probably sway somewhere between indifferent and unprintable. Indeed, this negative perception of banks is the strongest dynamic in the marketplace. Which is why the First Direct advertising strategy has, historically, looked to persuade the massed ranks of dissatisfied bank customers that there is a better option.

However, this is the story of how the development of a new campaign – fronted by the animated *Little Fella* – prompted us to realise that these dissatisfied customers weren't the most important audience for our advertising. Indeed, it became clear that the role of our advertising was less about persuasion and more about mobilisation, resulting in a further shift in creative direction that has produced a new and compelling First Direct campaign: *Magical Rapport.*

The potted strategy

First Direct is a niche brand in a world of giant global banking conglomerates with their equally giant and global marketing budgets. Worse still, First Direct has no High Street presence, which increases the pressure on the communication. Consequently, the marketing department is highly focussed on realistic objectives.

First Direct's acquisition strategy has always been to target high-value customers of other banks. More specifically, it is about targeting dissatisfied high-value customers of other banks. Whilst there are a fair few of these about, it's not as easy as one might hope. On average, changing banks happens less often than changing one's spouse. However, once First Direct has got its customer, he or she rarely leaves, for the simple reason that they're glad they moved.

All of which leads us to the role for the advertising, whose message could, until recently, be neatly summarised as: "Your bank is crap, First Direct isn't. Come and join us."

Of course there was a great deal more highly original and intellectual thinking than this statement suggests. Just like any other well organised brand-focussed client, First Direct has its collection of brand pyramids, onions and worlds, along with an armoury of brand visions, promises, values and tones. However, if you look back through the historical reel of advertising, the overall take-out is that First Direct is considerably less useless than everyone else.

It might not be rocket science, but when you're targeting a group of people who are dissatisfied it tends to make a great deal of sense. And it seemed to work[1].

The new work

As a client, First Direct has consistently produced excellent creative work. During the comparatively brief time it has existed it has also consistently varied its work. The reason for this is simple. If you're up against competitors with advertising budgets the size of GDPs, you'd better make sure you cut through.

In 1999 it was decided that a fresh campaign was required. The team went away and thought long and hard about what the brief should be, what was the essence of other banks' crapness? The resulting insight focussed on how, for most people, banks were a constant annoyance in their life. Banks were one of those uncomfortable background nuisances that never seem to quite go away. From this brief *Little Fella* was born.

A short little bald bloke

Little Fella was an animated character who walked along complaining about life's niggles – cheese and onion crisps in blue packets, people who stop right in front of you as you're walking along and the like. All in all he seemed to be a huge success. We liked him, the client liked him, Millward Brown thought he was okay (if only he'd tell people a bit more about the product), and to top it all the creative community liked him (the commercial won a golden arrow at the BTA Awards).

However, in amongst all this self-congratulation there were some worrying signs. Business results weren't looking very encouraging, new customers were down on targets. Was this new advertising too radical for our target audience? People started to get worried.

The consumer reaction

So *Little Fella* went into a fresh bout of research and the responses made us rethink.

When we spoke to our target market – those high-value dissatisfied customers of other banks – they thought the advertising was novel and fun. It also fitted well with their perceptions of First Direct – namely a little bit quirky and different. In summary, they felt it made you think that First Direct wasn't like the other banks, which was exactly the intention.

However, we also had a control sample of First Direct customers and their reaction was very different. They didn't like *Little Fella* at all. For them he represented the antithesis of exactly what they liked about their bank – its humanity. For them, it simply wasn't right to represent their beloved bank with a short funny looking bloke generated by a computer.

With this knowledge we went and had a look at some of First Direct's internal data – specifically customer recommendation and found it was falling off, dramatically. And this was worrying, because the biggest acquisition driver for First Direct is its own customer base. There were no internal reasons for this fall-off, customer service certainly hadn't deteriorated, if anything it had continued to get better. The inference was that this decline had to be a result of the advertising.

How the advertising really worked

This was a major revelation. Like any brand, we'd sought to develop advertising that our current customer base also enjoyed. However, it had never been a cornerstone of the strategic or creative development process, simply because they weren't the priority audience. Even so, to date it wasn't an issue, as we'd produced advertising that was liked by prospective and current customers alike.

Yet, we now had qualitative responses saying customers didn't like *Little Fella* and quantitative data showing declining recommendations. Our conclusion was that the current customer base felt less empowered to recommend First Direct because they didn't like the advertising. We realised that our supposed core audience of dissatisfied bank customers weren't as core as we'd thought.

Actually, our most important audience were the highly satisfied customers of First Direct, the people who didn't need to be told how wonderful their bank was, the people who certainly didn't need to know how rubbish other banks were. What they needed was the context for recommendation, they needed advertising which made them feel better about telling their friends how good First Direct really was. They needed mobilising.

The role of advertising was not to attract potential customers, it was to mobilise existing ones via a public forum. And First Direct now had over a million of these brand evangelists to let loose on the discontented consumers of rival banks.

Why First Direct customers love First Direct

If the advertising objective was now to rally our existing base, rather than address our potential customers, we needed to be communicating what they loved rather than what others hate.

The positives of First Direct aren't hard to find. As we've already seen, First Direct customers are massive brand advocates. However, the principal reason for this isn't, surprisingly, their 24 hour status. The principal reason customers love First Direct is the staff:

- "They're always friendly."

- "The staff are always very helpful and friendly."
- "They're all just so helpful."[2]

This isn't mere chance: First Direct has a recruitment policy that is committed to hiring nice people rather than banking people. Part of the recruitment process involves blind-folding potential employees, giving them a lemon to hold for one minute, putting that lemon in a box of other lemons and asking them to find their original lemon. It might seem a tad strange, but it's all part of training programme designed to intensify the senses in order to deliver a better customer experience.

The irony of First Direct is that, whilst they are known for being a telephone bank, they are most liked for being the most human of banks.

Fine tuning

Which was all fine and good. The problem is that everyone in banking is getting the same research. Research which says that consumers are fed up of bank closures and bored of dotcom banks and what they really want is some good old fashioned human contact.

The result is lots of warm, cuddly banking ads: "What can we do to make you happy?", "Our kind of people, your kind of bank". Enough to make consumers vomit and enough to make us slightly annoyed that everyone was encroaching on our territory.

So, we went back to our new, redefined role for advertising – what would motivate customers to recommend First Direct? It wasn't simply the fact that they were happy with First Direct. It wasn't simply that First Direct had great staff. Both of these told only half the story. What makes First Direct so different and so recommendable is the interaction between First Direct and its customers. Both sides get something back, it is very much a two-way relationship. This interaction is genuinely unique.

The brief

The rapport between bank and customer formed the basis of our brief:
- What are we advertising: the interaction between First Direct and its customers.
- Why are we advertising: to motivate First Direct customers to tell others about the joy of banking with First Direct.
- Target audience: First Direct customers.
- Proposition: First Direct understands that the relationship between staff and customers makes the difference.
- Support: the magic of a good rapport between individuals will make any situation more enjoyable and productive. That is why First Direct employs people who understand other people and why their customers are the most contented

banking customers in the UK.

The creative work

The brief resulted in a plethora of work, all of it strong. However, planning was able to provide further guidance during creative development.

Many of the ideas dramatised the customer-bank relationship by accentuating it. For example, the hairdresser whose love for his bank inspired him to give free haircuts to First Direct staff on their way to work. Or the customers who couldn't stop singing about their love of First Direct. However, customers didn't need advertising to spell out what made First Direct so special. First Direct customers are only too capable of describing in their own words why others should change bank, and the traditional over-promise of advertising would only undermine their conviction. The creative idea didn't so much have to say what made First Direct unique, as to allow customers to feel it.

What customers needed was advertising that prompted a smile, what they needed was a group of old men who can't stop laughing.

Conclusion

In the end, an advertisement on its own is never going to get people to do something as significant as buy a car, switch a mortgage or change banks. It is just one in a series of steps. What really makes people do things on big decisions such as these are the views of friends, those rambling pub conversations and general mutterings. What planning and the resulting *Magical Rapport* campaign has done is to help fire up a million mutterers to act as the delivery system for the campaign's effectiveness. Since the launch of *Magical Rapport*, recommend-ation levels at First Direct have soared, rising from 20% of responses pre-campaign to 36% post-campaign. In the world of planning, where the consumer insight is key, this is a case which shows how important it is to know who your target audience is first.

[1] First Direct won five stars at the IPA Effectiveness Awards in 1998.
[2] First Direct customers, David Douce Research April 2000

Campaigns for established service brands
sponsor: Denise Williams Executive Recruitment

Selling mascara by prescription

The key strategic breakthrough illustrated in this paper is the realisation that a key competitive strength of Boots as a retailer lies in the expertise of the pharmacist. Research led to the insight that whilst pharmacists are perceived by some to be dispensers of pills, ointments and cough mixture, the reality is that their expertise spans a wide range of issues throughout a person's life. This enables Boots to create a valuable relationship with their customers.

Winner: Fern Miller
Agency: J Walter Thompson
Creative Director: Will Awdry
Art Director: Alistair Wood
Copywriter: Alistair Wood
Client: Boots The Chemist
Product: Pharmacists

Introduction

This paper will show how planning recognised that chemists can sell more mascara than shopkeepers.

It will explain how planning persuaded a retailer to run advertising that couldn't sell anything.

It will illustrate how planning recognised that telling consumers something they had known about for years could still be new and surprising to them.

What seems to be the problem

At a time when retailer loyalty was dwindling and High Street prices were being slashed by bargain-hungry consumers, Boots as a brand was as close to the hearts of consumers as any business could hope to be. Most planners know the statistic by heart: in a survey conducted by the Henley Centre, people described Boots the Chemist as more trustworthy than the Government, the Church and the Royal Family[1].

But people were taking it for granted.

The symptoms

Talk to consumers about Boots and yes, they will happily eulogise about their trust and love for the brand. Talk to them about what Boots sells and they will tell you it's a bit dear, it's not very innovative, but it is dependable quality. 'Aha!' says the quack doctor, 'the answer is simple. They love the brand but the day-to-day product range and pricing is letting them down. Talk to them about what's new, talk to them about we have just launched, and most importantly, slash the prices!'

Of course a good doctor will look beyond the symptoms, and note down her own signs. She'll look for the presence of other symptoms, for links with other illnesses or syndromes historically. Of course you can treat the short term issues. Of course range and price are important. As much as treating the sniffles you get with a long-running cold, or the persistent cough of a smoker. But in the long run you have to build up your immune system, give up the nicotine.

The diagnosis: a powerful immune system

If you look at the history of how competitors have responded to Boots' strategy of either cutting prices or launching new products and services, you will find that from its first conception as a champion of bringing medicine to the people, through to the introduction of the first self-service Pharmacy, to Photo laboratories and own-brand cosmetics ranges, Boots has been a well-imitated innovator. And much as this is the greatest form of flattery, as soon as an innovation is copied, it no longer belongs to Boots.

Boots should never give up innovating, freshening, leading the way, it can only do so because underneath this activity is a strong foundation of trustworthiness.

It is blessed with a very powerful immune system. Where did that come from?

For instance, we knew it was the UK's number one cosmetics retailer, with the UK's number one brand of Cosmetics (No7). Something was keeping it buoyant in a very crowded market . It was being attacked from a wide range of angles – from the clinical, upmarket department store cosmetics counter, through to Superdrug's cheerfully funky High Street chain and lately, the grocery multiples' cheap and convenient burgeoning cosmetics and toiletries ranges.

And yet, when we talked to groups of cosmetics buyers, shoppers from all ends of the market told us that when it came to the sort of make-up they cared about – the mascara, foundations, powders and favourite lipsticks that they couldn't live without – they always went to Boots.

They could be standing by a shelf full of mascara in their local supermarket and they would go into town and get their mascara at a different time.

Like any behaviour that makes no sense at all, it intrigued the doctors in the planning department. So we asked a new set of make-up consumers what their first thoughts about Boots were – before we got them talking about the make-up Boots sells. The answer was obvious: the Chemist. What were their memories of Boots? The answer was clear. 'I bought some medicine for my littlest child the other day and the lady was so helpful.' 'The lady behind the counter told me about these new vitamins for smokers.' 'They seem to know about all sorts.'[2]

The professionalism, intimacy and reliability that Boots has come to stand for runs directly from their pharmacy. These healthcare credentials dig down a lot deeper than the news about current range and price promotions, and as long as the current range and price is kept in order, it's the chemist who will maintain the emotional bond consumers have with Boots. And when it comes to the mascara you can't live without, professionalism, intimacy and reliability build up the sort of values other cosmetics shopkeepers and manufacturers would kill for.

Boots was lucky, it was in its blood.

A history of good health

The superior trust shown in Boots over other British institutions is mirrored in the trust the public has in pharmacists. By comparison with other professionals a pharmacist is trusted to be more honest and fair than a GP, a bank, the Police or an MP[3] . Furthermore, in times when it is increasingly difficult to get time with a doctor, the desire to self-medicate means that people are ever more reliant on their pharmacist.

We realised that one of the key reasons for Boots being the leading health and beauty retailer was that people trust its pharmacists.

We understood that if we really wanted to pull out all the stops in claiming the high ground in this messy high street bunfight we would need to remind people about the pharmacists. No-one would ever say that they didn't know Boots had chemists, but didn't they need reminding that this was part of the reason they loved Boots?

Bitter medicine

Of course there was an immediate problem with this strategy: to maintain the professionalism that our pharmacists so scrupulously uphold, the advertising could not be seen to be selling medicines or other healthcare items.

Have you ever tried to persuade a retailer to run some television advertising that was precluded from selling anything?

Furthermore, the PAGB[4] Code of Practice disallows advertising that claims one pharmacist, or group of pharmacists are better than another. So we couldn't even claim superior training, listening skills, or service. It was beginning to seem that there wasn't much we could say.

Our initial thought was this: due to the scale of the Boots network we could surprise people with facts and figures: Boots has 1,950 pharmacists, 2,600 health-care assistants, prints 4,400,000 leaflets on healthcare on 21 different subjects. That's all pretty impressive.

We'll need to do some tests

In order to understand the full scope of the role that Boots' pharmacists have in the nation's health, we interviewed pharmacists in stores throughout the country and asked them about what they did, day to day.

We showed them some ideas. How about we do some advertising that dramatises just how many customers you see every day? Or how many different subjects you know about? After all, we have been talking to consumers and they tell us how surprised they are by your range of expertise – would this reflect your job? 'Yes', said the pharmacists, 'that is true.' The numbers looked impressive. But they didn't look very impressed.

So we asked them what made their job fulfilling and unsurprisingly it wasn't how many prescriptions they wrote or leaflets they had to give out. They talked about the ability to listen and advise, to build up relationships with their customers even if it's just for a few minutes. To identify the real problems and then provide solutions. To manage a teenager's asthma, to cure a young child's rash, to help someone give up smoking. We began to see a way in which telling people old news could still be surprising. Had anyone really brought to life what pharmacists do?

We talked to customers who used the service and we talked to people who hadn't used it for a while. We made some key discoveries:

1. Those who haven't used the service of a pharmacist for a while tend to think

of them as the nice people who give them cough medicine when they've got a cold, dispense ointment for nasty rashes and perhaps advise you on something for a touch of Delhi belly.

2. People who use the service more regularly (people with children, older people and those with long term health difficulties) rely on the pharmacist for everyday support. They turn to the pharmacist first when their toddler develops a worrying cough, when they don't want to trouble the doctor with their gammy knee, when they need some more of the medicine that manages chronic pain. This everyday support is not trivial, as the previous group might think. It's a constant source of relief and advice.

3. What pharmacists don't tell you is that they deliver oxygen to the dying. That they advise on the menopause. That they provide pain relief for labour pains. That they can help you quit smoking. That the range of issues they know about is much broader than you'd expect.

Advertising would be able to show that each incident in which the pharmacist has helped with a problem joins up, to become a lifetime of support. We wanted to bring these solutions close to home, and make them recognisable. If this film was going to have a positive effect on brand loyalty we needed it trigger memories of trust, affection and optimism for the Boots pharmacist. And importantly, by dramatising the ultimate results of the visit to the pharmacist, we could surprise people a little with a service that was a hundred years old.

The treatment

We had established:

1. That advertising the pharmacist would have a halo effect on our overall brand.

2. That for this advertising to claim the Boots' pharmacists' rightful position as healthcare authorities we would have to take them beyond tummy aches, rashes and colds in the public's perception.

3. That not only should the advertising dramatise a range of seriousness in problems, it should also dramatise the way in which that support is felt *throughout* a person's life.

4. That this should be executed in such a way as to inspire warm feelings of optimism, affection and trust in the viewer, not the cold sentiments of respect or admiration (which we had enough of already).

A prescription

Our research had told us that the most important task of this advertising was to turn 'everyday support' from the trivial to the faithful. So our brief to the creative department was this: dramatise the full scope of the role that Boots plays in the nation's health, from the minor to the major, from cradle to grave.

We talked to the creatives about the range of drama in the issues that the pharmacist helps with – from the chronic and painful right through to the temporary and uncomfortable. They were, naturally, drawn to one end of the scale and their initial work focussed on the hard-hitting drama that people don't realise that pharmacists get involved in: drug abuse or delivering oxygen to the dying.

But our understanding of the relationship between pharmacist and customer had told us that it was just as important to trigger memories that the viewer can relate to, and actually, if it was brought to life, the pain of a little boy's grazed knee, or the anxiety relating to your wife's menopause was much more powerful than someone else's hypodermic needle.

Surprising results

Bearing in mind how frequently a person pops into a chemist in their lifetime and how familiar and dependable the Boots pharmacy is, it may surprise one to discover that 67% of people who saw the advertising for the pharmacy felt it was 'new and surprising for Boots' [5]. 78% described it as 'fresh' and 69% said it 'made you feel Boots was up to date'.[6]

But that goes to show that when the familiar is reappraised, surprising success can follow.

[1] Henley Centre 'Planning for Consumer Change', 1998
[2] JWT qualitative cosmetics research, 2000
[3] Ibid
[4] Proprietary Association of Great Britain. The trade association that represents manufacturers of over-the-counter medicines and food supplements.
[5] Base: all purchasing from Boots in the last 12 months (Cla) and recognising telepic, Source: Boots Brand Tracking survey, Research International
[6] Ibid

Campaigns for established product brands

The APG Creative Planning Awards

TV: Any food tastes supreme with Heinz salad cream

Ambient media

Print

GOLD
Leo Burnett

Campaigns for established product brands
sponsor: Express Train

Never say die:
the revival of Heinz Salad Cream

Heinz Salad Cream was a relic from an era of limp salads. But planning saw an opportunity to reintroduce it to a new generation as an anarchic way of livening-up everyday dull foods, boldly breaking the rules of food advertising along the way. Planning spotted a way to re-position Heinz Salad Cream radically, moving right away from salads.

Winners: Sharon Masnick, Mark Stockdale
Agency: Leo Burnett
Creative Directors: Nick Bell, Mark Tutssel
Art Director: Rob Neilson
Copywriter: Jack Stephens
Client: Heinz
Product: Heinz Salad Cream

Background

Invented in 1914, Heinz Salad Cream became a great British icon.

Which was its problem.

By 1980 it symbolised the 'Great British salad': lukewarm lettuce, soggy tomato, dry cucumber – the sort of thing you'd had to endure back in the 60s and 70s at some aged Aunt's house. Think doilies.

The British palette had evolved. Travel and an ever-growing range of cosmopolitan restaurants raised our expectations. Our appetite for salad cream diminished as our salads became more adventurous, and we traded up to 'sophisticated' mayonnaise (it's French, you know) and a variety of exotic ready-made dressings.

So it was hardly a surprise when, in late 1998, a portfolio review conducted by a well-known management consultancy recommended that Heinz de-list salad cream.

Discussions ensued. For all its problems, Heinz Salad Cream was still a cherished member of the portfolio. But corporate nostalgia is rarely the best business strategy. So, could the category be turned around?

What would it cost? Lots, presumably. In fact, client and agency estimated we'd need roughly a 70% price increase to fund even a moderate weight of advertising without completely wrecking the brand's P&L!

The debate boiled down to this: if the salad cream category can be turned round at the same time as we virtually double Heinz's price, let's do it. But that's a pretty big 'if'.

Thoughts, agency? "We'll get back to you in the New Year", said the planners.

Dead end one: existing users

One obvious place to look for new volume was existing users – might they use more?

Planning wasn't convinced. Users, typically 40+ C2DE's with limited disposable incomes, were already very heavy consumers with firmly entrenched habits. Far from being open to new uses for salad cream, surely they'd be more likely to desert Heinz after a 70% price rise? Besides, to re-build the category don't we need to target younger consumers?

Dead end two: Heinz mums

As we dismissed existing users, a strong consensus formed around targeting core heartland Heinz loyalists - young families with kids, who are already using other Heinz products (beans, spaghetti, soup, etc).

Clearly, they're younger than existing salad cream users, and families offer serious volume potential. Experience with other Heinz products had also shown that, if mum and dad used salad cream, they'd introduce it to their kids, who'd then adopt it for life.

So, maybe we could build on their existing relationship with the brand and cross-promote salad cream on the back of other products in the portfolio?

The trouble was it only took a handful of groups to show what little chance we had with these people. Today's Heinz mums have grown up in the 'Mayonnaise Age' and remembered salad cream from their maiden aunts in the '60s and '70s. No, no, this generation is too cosmopolitan, too 'today' for salad cream.

Right. We'd just met the 'Mayo Bigots' and we were stuck.

New horizons

Now, it may not have escaped your notice that lots of young people work in advertising agencies. And many of these people (I know you'll be shocked, dear reader) often go out socialising until late at night – sometimes drinking alcohol, we've heard – and live in slightly chaotic flats with chaotic eating habits to match.

Being a friendly couple of planners, we occasionally mingle with these youngsters. And sitting in just such a young person's flat, chatting away one night, something struck us.

The topic was 'Appalling Things I Have Done Since Living On My Own', and shocking stories about food had turned out to be a recurring theme. And thus it occurred to us that when you first start living on your own you eat (to use a technical term) an extraordinary amount of crap.

Poking our noses in

So, sniffing the germ of a strategic idea, we started nosing around young people's kitchens – brothers, sisters, friends, colleagues, anyone, we weren't proud.

Almost every twentysomething we knew appeared to exist on takeaways and bland, easy-to-prepare carbohydrates – baked potato, pasta, baked potato, cheese on toast, baked potato, microwave chips, baked potato.

Surely, we reasoned excitedly, wouldn't a dash of Heinz Salad Cream transform such dull crap into something altogether more scintillating?
Moreover, aren't they young enough not to have encountered salad cream in the past and so won't be carrying any negative baggage? And haven't they yet to settle-down into any long term eating habits? So presumably, then, won't they have more open minds than the 'Mayo Bigots'?

Nonetheless, a couple of things did worry us: we knew this age group was the least likely to have a relationship with the Heinz brand; and more open-minded though we hoped they would be, the reality was that not only had they never considered salad cream, they were actually perfectly happy doing what they were doing without it. Perhaps we'd better go and talk to them properly, we decided, before we get too carried away.

Do whatever you like

There was little point just convening a few groups of young twentysomethings (it's hardly as if they've got anything to tell us about salad cream, is it?), so instead we decided to test our hypothesis that 'they eat lots of dull food and Heinz Salad Cream ought to be able to add some taste to it.'

So, inspired by our evening swapping stories with mates, we tried to recreate the same kind of dynamic by recruiting friendship groups (about six friends per group) and gave them each a bottle of Heinz Salad Cream. "Go away", we said, "and do whatever you like with this."

A week later they came back and swapped stories about what they'd got up to. Quite spontaneously, they'd found uses ranging from the unusual (adding a bit of zest to a fry-up) to the bizarre (Branston Pickle and Heinz Salad Cream mixed together with crisps, served on toast, anyone?).

We asked them why they'd done these things. And they told us they'd found salad cream added loads of flavour to their dull food. Hurrah! (And, rather conveniently, it also turned out they had no idea how much a bottle cost! Double hurrah!!)

However pleasing though this affirmation was, what they did with salad cream wasn't the only thing that caught our imagination. It wasn't just what they said, but it was how they said it.

It was as if they were competing to tell the most disgusting story – just like what had happened at our young friend's flat a few months before. OK, at times they were a little embarrassed, and they all joined in the mock outrage, but we strongly suspected these people were really proud of their ability to consume odd food-stuffs, getting a kick out of being as unconventional as possible.

In short, we believed this was young people doing what young people invariably do – trying to be different from the 'rest of us'.

Boy, thought the planners, can the creatives have some fun with this insight.

At last – a strategy

The proposition couldn't have been simpler. We wanted to tell young twenty-somethings – just setting up home, living on dull carbohydrates – that 'Heinz Salad Cream protects your food from being boring'.

There was no support needed, other than to show food that would otherwise be unappetising being made yummy by Heinz Salad Cream. This had nothing to do with salad.

And crucially, we asked the creatives to go for a tone-of-voice that captured the "oh you didn't, you couldn't have …!" that we'd heard in the stories being swapped at our mate's flat and in our friendship groups.

The creative idea

To say the creatives literally executed the brief would be to demean the quality of their work. The brilliance was in the simplicity and purity of the idea: people using Heinz Salad Cream to make all sorts of unpalatable things taste fantastic, with a no nonsense strap line – 'Any food tastes supreme with Heinz Salad Cream'.

But it was the anarchic tone of voice we'd asked for – the "that's nothing, I once …" – that pushed them to take this idea to its logical conclusion. And the result was advertising that was as far from the conventional, clichéd approach of 'romancing the food' as it was possible to be.

These ads showed people nonchalantly making edible all manner of things that were downright disgusting.

A near-death experience

As recommendations go, this was a major, nerve-jangling leap for Heinz. Research was deemed essential. And this, unfortunately, almost killed the strategy and the creative idea.

Based largely on responses to the question "how would you improve this campaign", the researcher argued that because the campaign was so different from 'typical' Heinz advertising, it needed to be made more 'Heinzy' in the interests of brand synergy. The debrief also worried about associating the product with unpalatable food, and instead recommended we demonstrate how Heinz Salad Cream tastes great on modern foods like tacos and curries. Furthermore, "the product should be the hero – rather than using it to resurrect food, people should be shown looking for any excuse to enjoy it."

Effectively all our thinking and the resulting creative work was being thrown out. But every instinct told us to reject these conclusions. So we swapped our 'planner hats' for our 'researcher hats' and set about going back over the group transcripts with a fine tooth-comb.

We felt the researcher's analysis overlooked the respondents' initial surprise and hilarity when they first saw the idea; that it ignored their astonishment at seeing advertising like this from Heinz, and the positive impact this astonishment had had on their view of the brand; that no allowance was made of the way they immediately understood the strategy and recognised and enjoyed the hyperbole.

Encouragingly, the client accepted these arguments. But, the real sticking point was what people had actually said when asked the question, "how would you improve this campaign …?" For example: "… well, that one does make me feel a bit queasy …", "… done like this, these aren't very Heinzy …"

So, planning argued that people can't answer this question meaningfully – a layman hauled in off the street is in no way qualified to write (let alone re-write) ads.

I kind of agree, said the client, but that doesn't change the fact that respondents did talk about feeling queasy and so forth.

And so we went round all the obvious debates: we need advertising that leaves people feeling a little uncomfortable otherwise it'll just end up as wallpaper, comments about 'Heinz-ness' are being conditioned by past preconceptions – precisely what the advertising has to challenge and so on...

Lots of nodding from our client, but those damn quotes just wouldn't go away. Queasy. Not Heinz.

In amongst all the debating, though, a 'researchery' thought kept nagging at the back of our plannery minds: the respondents in our friendship groups had been vying to outdo each other with their 'revolting' stories, just like our mates in the flat that night, whereas the respondents in the focus groups appeared highly conservative. Self-consciously so.

And then it struck us: re-do the research with friendship groups, in-home. Then they can talk freely about the kinds of things they get up to, without feeling any embarrassment in front of randomly recruited strangers, let alone in front of whoever might be lurking behind that two-way mirror! Hopefully they will respond to the advertising more honestly.

A new researcher came on-board, discussed the advertising idea brilliantly with four friendship groups, and the rest, as they say, is history.

History in the making

This campaign has won 25 major creative awards – including Cannes Silver, Creative Circle, BTAA and Eurobest.

Advertising awareness and brand consideration grew enormously amongst our new target audience.

Despite the 70% price rise, a 40+% share was held.

But more importantly, within one summer of the re-launch, new young users accounted for 25% of Heinz Salad Cream purchasers.

Cinema/TV:

"Six chances"

"Coffee!"

"Peanut"

GOLD
D'Arcy

Campaigns for established product brands
sponsor: Express Train

Eating Revels is a risky business

Planning identified that Revels' apparent product weakness was in fact the key to consumers' positive relationship with the brand. Revels was a dormant brand with unexploited nostalgia value. People's first memories of Revels centred on the flavours they claimed to dislike violently, but there was also extreme enthusiasm about the flavours they did like. The key thing about eating Revels is that, unlike eating anything else, it's a risky business.

Winner: Robert Tansey
Agency: D'Arcy
Creative Director: Nick Hastings
Art Director: David Childlow
Copywriter: Matt Wheeler
Client: Masterfoods
Product: Revels

Introduction

This is a story of how groundbreaking confectionery advertising came from planning's recognition that Revels' apparent product failing was, in fact, the key to the whole eating experience.

There's bags more for everyone!

In 1999, nostalgia hit the chocolate world to great effect. Both Fry's Turkish Delight and Cadbury's Flake went on air with old advertising and witnessed significant increases in sales.

Not wanting to miss out on a seemingly easy win, Mars identified Revels (a bag containing a variety of chocolate sweets) as the product in their portfolio that could mimic this success. It, too, was a dormant brand, whose imagery and associations had never really left the 1970s and one whose advertising archive must surely have harboured a nostalgia-laden gem.

Unfortunately not. After much searching we only managed to unearth one, very average commercial: on a set of balancing scales, the variety of sweets offered by Revels outweighs a similar bag of ordinary, one flavour chocolates, accompanied by the distinctly unedifying proclamation that 'there's bags more for everyone!'

This ad just didn't seem to have the requisite emotional content to provoke a nostalgic return to Revels among our consumers and we took the collective decision with the client not to run it.

This decision did not, however, negate the fact that Revels was a dormant brand with great growth potential and that it just needed a kick start to reawaken people's affection for it. As a result, we were asked to write a new brief for work that would truly lead to consumers reconnecting emotionally with Revels.

The good, the bad and the orange

As sales of Revels had stabilised at fairly low levels, it was quite difficult to find regular eaters with whom we could talk. Because Revels have been around for ages, however, we had no difficulty locating people in their twenties and thirties – a key market for bitesize products – who not only remembered having eaten them, but were only too keen to express an opinion.

At face value, what we heard was extremely discouraging. Everybody, but everybody immediately remembered virulently disliking one of the flavours. It seemed that the mere mention of Revels sparked a pavlovian diatribe on on how disgusting that particular sweet was.

It wasn't all bad, however. For once they'd got the pent up vitriol to these particular flavours off their chests, they were just as extreme in their ecstatic recollections of the flavours they'd absolutely adored.

For a moment we thought that maybe the solution lay first in the manu-facturing process, rather than at the door of an advertising agency. Surely Mars should reconfigure the selection to include only sweets which people so patently remembered adoring? This moment of marketing revelation was, however, just that: a moment. For when the team pooled their findings, it became clear that there wasn't one single universally-hated sweet. Some people hated coffee, while others blanched at the recollection of orange, coconut or raisin. It looked like we'd have to recommend wholesale changes to the product line-up if we were to pursue this route.

This, of course, would have been utter folly, because of the old adage that one man's nectar is another man's poison. Whereas lots of people said they loathed coffee, some professed it to be their favourite (subsequent quantitative validation of this showed that, while coffee is the most disliked, it is also the favourite sweet of 20% of Revels devotees) and orange seemed to have equal numbers of supporters and detractors.

So where did we go from here with an out of date brand, with sweets in it that people claimed to hate?

Indifference is the greatest insult

It was at this point that planning made another breakthrough when relistening to the research tapes. Having moderated or sat in on endless groups, all good planners know they've got a dud ad, strategy or product on their hands when the material presented is met with the 'I suppose it's OK' type of indifference. What was remarkable about the way people talked about Revels was the complete lack of indifference on show. The pendulum was always swinging, in the same person, from extreme hatred to extreme enthusiasm. There was definite excitement on show. People simply loved talking about Revels.

These reactions got us thinking again, because surely a bag of ordinarily flavoured sweets didn't merit such a reaction? After all, we were only talking about coffee, toffee, peanut and the like, not paint stripper, vomit and ambrosia. What was it about Revels that generated such exaggerated reactions? Why were people so excited?

It was here that planning identified two key reasons: one that was related to the product and one that was a function of Revels being a brand from people's childhood. Both would directly influence the creative brief.

Eeny meeny, miny, mo

When you're given a box of variety chocolates, the selection card, the wrappers and the pretty designs on the sweets themselves give you the luxury of being able to choose the ones you like and avoid the ones you don't.

With Revels, however, there are no such clues as to which sweet might be which. In fact, with the exception of the Minstrel type sweet, they are all round and covered in milk chocolate. But they aren't absolutely identical, they are only nearly identical. This, we observed, has a great effect on how people eat Revels. Knowing that there are some sweets they like more than others, people often spend a considerable amount of time choosing which they are going to eat next: comparing sizes (the Maltesers are often slightly larger); checking the relative weights (the peanut can be slightly lighter than the fondant centres); sniffing them for faint traces of coffee or orange; or even just playing childish selection games like eeny, meeny, miny, mo.

This active selection process is entirely different from that of any other sweet, where you always know what you're putting in your mouth. With Revels, however, you can never be 100% certain that the sweet you've chosen is the one you think it is. This wouldn't really matter if you liked all the flavours, but, as we knew, everybody hates at least one. The presence of the sweets people don't like therefore introduces a huge element of risk into the eating experience. It might be their favourite sweet, but, then again, it might be their worst.

It was obviously this element of risk that was causing so much excitement when people talked about Revels. Not having eaten the product for so long, they were unable to articulate it clearly, but we realised that the very presence of the bad sweets was entirely central to to the Revels brand. Without them, they'd just be another bag of sweets. With them, eating Revels becomes risky and generates the extreme emotional response we'd been witnessing.

What we'd initially thought was a product failing was now integral to the advertising brief and the proposition – eating Revels is a risky business – was one we felt sure would prove to be creatively fertile.

I'm sure Mars Bars used to be bigger than they are now

We were very excited about our proposition, but we wanted to make sure that it directed the creatives in such a way as to exploit the fact that the brand was one that people remembered fondly (albeit strangely) from their childhood and adolescence. We needed to ensure that their nostalgia gland was aroused in the right way.

It was while musing on the nature of nostalgia that planning identified the second reason for people's amplified reactions towards Revels. The fact about nostalgia and reminiscence is that memories tend to get exaggerated over time. The one vaguely sunny holiday in Cornwall becomes a two week heatwave. School dinners go from unappetising to not being fit for animals. Anna Glover becomes a vision of celestial beauty rather than the only plain little twelve year old that let you kiss her at the bus stop.

The way our lapsed eaters were talking about Revels fitted equally into this pattern. Though now mature adults, they were still over-reacting to the flavours in the way they thought they did as children. So, in order to maximise this memory, it was going to be important that the advertising somehow harked back to our target audience's past as well as dramatising the essential risk inherent in eating Revels.

Has he fired six shots or only five?

Mars dominates the bitesize category through Maltesers and we were obviously keen for any uplift in sales of Revels not to have a detrimental effect on this business. The bitesize category is also predominantly female and we saw in Revels the opportunity for attracting men and therefore avoiding cannibilisation of Maltesers. Men were a particularly appropriate target given the puerility of the extreme reactions generated by the eating of Revels. Yes, women had expressed similar reactions to the men we'd talked to, but the latter reacted much more virulently and seemed more involved in the intricate ways of choosing the sweets.

The creative briefing session, therefore, had three main tasks: to remind the team of the inherent risk in eating Revels; to highlight the relevance of nostalgia; and to ensure a male emphasis in the advertising. This was packaged up into a short briefing film comprising iconic moments of risk and choice with which every self-respecting twentysomething man would be intimately acquainted: Dirty Harry asking the punk if he thinks he's fired six shots or only five; James Bond choosing which wire to remove from the ticking bomb; or the Cincinnati Kid trying to decide whether to fold or raise.

A bullet in the chamber

On a good day, briefs are able to stimulate an immediate creative solution and, in this case, the team went from our iconic moments to one of their own – and one which got even closer to the experience of eating Revels: the Russian Roulette scene from *The Deer Hunter*. Here they had found a perfect vehicle. It could show the agony of choice and the inherent risk involved. It also provided a perfect backdrop against which to perform the ludicrously exaggerated reactions we wanted to show when people get the right and wrong sweets - what could be more exaggerated than the threat of death and gambling Vietnamese? And it recalled a scene that would have left an indelible imprint on the minds of our target audience.

It's a bullseye

We were able to add another element of nostalgia to the media through planning spots in reruns of 70s classics and on specialist channels such as Bravo. But the cinema was to be our trump card. Although only 10% of Revels sales now go through these outlets, many people strongly associate them with early trips to the cinema and our 90-second epic is the perfect vehicle for hotwiring this association.

Unfortunately, budget cuts have pushed almost all of the air time back to 2002 and we have not yet had the opportunity to air the 30-second commercial or one of the 10-second variants, but we have work that we hope will win creative awards and a proposition that has provided innumerable ideas for point-of-sale material, promotional mechanics and on-line gaming. Risky business is clearly an area of immense fertility and one which fits perfectly with the Revels eating experience.

SILVER
Fallon

Campaigns for established product brands
sponsor: Express Train

Flowers and plants are good for you

Applying rigour and inventiveness hand in hand, planning got to the bottom of the real problem in the market and the real opportunity. Identifying the right audience and media along the way, planning's rigorous analysis of the product benefits provided a surprising but sound springboard for highly original creative work.

Winner: Nikki Crumpton
Agency: Fallon
Creative Directors: Richard Flintham, Andy McLeod
Art Director: Richard Flintham
Copywriter: Andy McLeod
Client: Flowers & Plants Association
Product: Flowers & Plants Association

Background

The Flowers and Plants Association is the organisation responsible for the generic promotion of flowers and plants in the UK. Its budget is small and, despite the superficial attractiveness of the category, creative cut-through is an absolute must.

This paper charts a surprisingly brutal path of strategic exploration and reductionism which genuinely led the client and our creatives not only to a strategy they would never instinctively have travelled to, but also to a celebrated print campaign.

Defining the problem

Let's start at the beginning, which was to properly define the problem.

The data provided to us by the Flowers and Plants Association portrayed a very healthy business picture. Here was a market experiencing growth on a yearly basis. However, when we looked at the sales data on a monthly basis, the market showed dramatic peaks and troughs around certain times of the year. And this was a pattern that had not changed over a number of years.

It seemed that despite its growth the market had underlying structural problems that, if addressed, could grow the market more substantially. The easy route would be to grow the peaks further, but this wouldn't tackle the structural problem. It could also deepen existing business problems for both suppliers and retailers. We felt that the strategy lay in understanding the troughs, and what was causing them.

So what was the data actually telling us?

Well it was obvious that this was a market that had some key dates in its calendar: Valentine's Day, Easter, Mother's Day, and to a lesser extent Christmas. But this seasonality was just the symptom of an underlying problem.

The real problem was the way consumers interacted with the product.

What the sales data had given us was a glimpse into the psyche of the British. But it took further investigation into market data to reveal this characteristic more clearly. The market data reinforced the stereotype that we Brits are in fact an emotionally stunted nation. Since Victorian times we have used flowers as a handy shortcut for voicing our emotions, and all the communication to date had reinforced those behaviour patterns ('Say it with flowers' being a classic example).

Drilling down further into the data we discovered more evidence to support our theory. The top ten reasons for buying flowers were dominated by occasions where one might want to express some sort of emotion. The top three were to congratulate someone on their birthday, as a thank you on Mother's Day and to say 'sorry' for a funeral. Then came hospital visiting, then spur of the moment purchase, followed by a thank you purchase when visiting friends or relations. The remaining five included cheering someone up, as a thank you present, to cheer yourself up, as a St Valentine's gift and as a romantic gesture.

This is where we differ from our European cousins, for whom flowers are as much a staple on the shopping list as bread or milk, and their steadier sales curves are testament to this. Because of this emotional baggage, consumers in this country find it very hard to picture flowers as a purchase that could potentially exist on a more everyday level.

In fact, of the 87% of the population that purchased flowers over a year only 13% of people said they bought flowers regularly, not for an occasion. This was a huge opportunity. Our strategy needed to focus on driving frequency rather than penetration.

And so we came to a strategic fork in the road.

Developing the strategy

One route to go down could be "the everyday special occasion', in order to get people to buy more flowers. However, we instinctively felt this was not a differentiating enough strategy to trigger a behavioural change. (Nor did it feel like an especially surprising or fertile creative start point).

If the problem in the market was one of usage, the role for us surely had to be to try and persuade people not to relegate flowers and plants to highdays and holidays, and this was where we decided to go with the truly differentiating route. We would get people to buy them more regularly by giving people rational reasons to purchase to complement the emotional reasons that currently drove the market.

We now felt we had the beginnings of a really interesting strategy. But this was where the task became harder. How could we change centuries of conditioning as to the role of flowers in our culture, and what precisely did we mean by 'rational reasons to buy'? We started to root around in books and on the internet for articles that treated flowers and plants differently from the way people were currently using them.

Testing the approach

The first justification for this approach came in the form of a quote which pointed to the physiological and psychological effects of plants and flowers as a potential rational route:

'Flowers and plants are more than things we send people when they are ill, as a gift, token of affection, or expression of sorrow. Flowers and plants can and do heal us, both emotionally and physically, with their smell, their very existence and their beauty' (*The Language of Flowers* by Krystyna Arcarti)

We now needed evidence to support this quote, and our client was able to help. NASA had carried out a study on the ability of plants to clean the air we breathe, thus reducing our ingestion of harmful chemicals. When quizzed, our client furnished us with even more of these sorts of facts, adding further grist to our strategic mill.

Slowly we started building up a body of evidence to support our theory. Our information gathering spread round the globe, with emails flying across continents to professors, lecturers, researchers, drug companies, colour theorists and feng shui experts, as to the beneficial properties of plants and flowers.

We ended up with a list of rational reasons to purchase flowers that would help people to see flowers and plants as good things to have around on an everyday basis, not just for special occasions. Facts such as:
- Reduction of noise pollution (plants)
- Removal of harmful chemicals (plants)
- Promotion of feelings of relaxation (flowers)
- Alleviating symptoms of SAD (flowers)
- Aiding concentration (plants and flowers)
- Prevention of colds and flu (plants).

Towards a creative brief

So what did all these facts add up to and how did we turn quite dry research facts into an interesting brief?

At some point the creative planning process has to start closing itself down. We had defined the problem creatively, decided to solve it with a truly differentiating route; we now needed to employ simplification to achieve a creatively-focussed proposition. All the facts seemed to point to one simple truth: that plants and flowers are good for you. So this was the proposition that we used on the brief.

However, we needed to revisit the audience again, for two reasons.

In search of a target audience

Was it a strategy that had any meaning for anyone? And because our budget was so small, what segment of the population would it be most relevant for?

We tackled first things first. Was this strategy just a bit too Haight-Ashbury for consumers? Apparently not. We were in fact riding the crest of the zeitgeist with this positioning. There had been an unparalleled recent growth in the belief that natural is best. Yoga, vitamin pills and herbal remedies were all the rage; housewives in Solihull as well as media types in London were taking up relaxation techniques and alternative therapies.   Britain was starting to experiment with a natural and holistic approach to life on a mass market, mainstream level, and we decided to ride the coat tails of these trends.

But whom should we target, in order that our budget went as far as it could go? Initially we looked again at the existing market's demographic make up, but this proved to be a bit of a red herring.

At the extreme (e.g. birthday buyers) the market was almost demographically flat across age, class and region. At best we got to 25 to 54 year old ABC1's, which was still way too broad a target for both creative and media people. The only critical area of distinction was sex, which really didn't come as any surprise. Our audience was emphatically women.

Within the universe of women we decided that the softest target audience for our activity was those who had begun to use flowers and plants differently, but who were not yet regular, non-occasion-led purchasers. And it was here that we found a more meaningful demographic distinction. They were working.

But did this mean they were open to our message? They might be starting to buy flowers and plants differently but would they appreciate the way in which we were presenting new news? We decided to look at the stuff they were interested in, the magazines they were consuming, programmes they were watching, and what they were spending their money on.

We felt vindicated as we ploughed through articles on well-being, achieving natural balance, and utilising nature's remedies to achieve optimum health. This also meant that by default we had selected our media.

Our creative target audience therefore resolved itself as working women who already buy flowers on impulse or for themselves, and our media audience was working women aged 25 to 45 who regularly read a women's glossy.

Our brief was now complete.

The creative brief
● Role for advertising: encourage working women to buy plants and flowers more regularly, by balancing their emotional allure with more rational reasons to purchase.
● Target audience: working women who already buy flowers and plants on impulse but not regularly.
● These women love articles on well-being, personal grooming and health. We will be targeting them in monthly magazines.
● Proposition: flowers and plants are good for you.
● Support: we have discovered facts that support this view, and we would like people to know about them so they don't just relegate plants and flowers to emotional gift-giving.

The creative strategy
As with most strategies, they don't come alive fully until you see the creative expression of them. For what had seemed such a classic planning approach, there was a fear that we had been too process-driven to arrive at a truly creative brief.

However we were not to be disappointed.

The creative route surprisingly did not show one plant or flower, and this was its inherent strength.

The treatment comprised beautifully-shot everyday scenarios (children playing in a front room, someone lying in bed with a cold, a young woman looking suitably rough after a night on the tiles) with our 'flower facts' sitting where flowers and plants might have. This wasn't a mere creative quirk, qualitative research later confirmed that the executions made people aware of their own 'gaps' that needed to be filled.

We wouldn't be able to claim this paper as a tribute to rigorous creative planning without the appearance of qualitative research. We researched the creative in order to double-check that this strategy wasn't too radical or marginal to make a difference, and were pleasantly surprised by how hard it worked. Our target really liked the facts and the new news, but they liked it because they now felt they were armed with ammunition to destroy the feelings of guilt they often got when purchasing (particularly flowers) for themselves. Emotion really was the driving force in this market, and not always positively, but our choice of using the rational to counterbalance the emotional seemed to be a really good way of eradicating the real emotional barrier to regular purchase: guilt.

The media

To make the money go as far as it could, we ran the executions in women's monthlies, in and around the well-being pages. But the more impressive element of media was the attention we got on the PR front. By riding the zeitgeist, we were providing journalists with a great story, particularly as the support was backed up by credible research sources.

We had unwittingly written a great springboard for creative PR efforts, not just creative advertising efforts.

The PR spanned a number of different media (including TV), not just PR in our chosen medium (magazines). This incremental publicity resulted in 13 million people seeing some form of communication about flowers and plants beyond our tightly-defined audience.

In summary

An original, dramatic and thought-provoking advertising solution prompted wholly by robust but inspired strategic thinking.

SILVER
Fallon

Campaigns for established product brands
sponsor: Express Train

Confronting prejudice: Skoda's rebirth

Planning's contribution to the inspired creative work that transformed Skoda's fortunes was to provide a definition of the problem that enabled everyone to look at it with different eyes. The biggest barrier to buying a Skoda was irrational prejudice against the brand. The role for advertising therefore had to be to confront that prejudice, not just in potential purchasers but in others perpetuating the prejudice.

Winner: David Hall
Agency: Fallon
Creative Directors: Richard Flintham, Andy McLeod
Art Director: Richard Flintham
Copywriter: Andy McLeod
Client: Skoda UK
Product: Fabia

Introduction

It is a truth universally acknowledged that an ambitious APG submission must be in possession of the following:

- A thorny problem.
- An innovative research programme revealing a killer insight.
- An inspired proposition leading directly to the creative work.

Unsurprisingly, planning tends to be the hero, and other contributors to the process take more minor roles.

This paper will take a slightly different approach.

The Skoda campaign is well known to be effective (actually in a rather old fashioned advertising-driven way). It is also highly creative for its category. The credit for much of this undeniably lies with an inspired creative leap. Planning was by no means the star of this show. This, however, is the story of how planning played an invisible but crucial role in getting the creatives to a point where such a leap was possible.

In addition, this paper will touch on two styles of planning – a logical research-based method that had actually begun to hold Skoda back and then the fresher, more intuitive approach that enabled us to propel the brand forward.

I hope to demonstrate that different planning challenges require different approaches. Classic planning, with its emphasis on research and craft skills, isn't always appropriate. While the application of fresh thinking and intuition to hard problems – sometimes unfairly dismissed as 'Gonzo planning', often is.

Background

You're probably pretty familiar with the basics of Skoda's brand problem. It started with shiploads of tinny cars, imported from the Eastern bloc in the 70s and 80s and sold at bargain-basement prices. Yet somewhere along the way this shoddy, unassuming car turned into a national obsession. Skoda was a laughing stock – spawning a series of jokes that were repeated in pubs, offices and playgrounds up and down the country. My personal favourite is the one about why Skodas have heated rear windscreens (answer: to keep your hands warm while you are pushing them).

If the Skoda product was bad, the brand's image was off the scale. Skoda found themselves cornered, serving an eccentric niche of budget drivers who took a perverse pleasure in the derision they attracted. A day out for the Skoda Owners Club could easily be mistaken for an excursion from the local funny farm.

All this would probably still be the case now, had it not been for a small historical event in the form of the fall of communism and the dismantling of the iron curtain.

In 1991 Skoda became part of the VW Group and a dramatic modernisation process began. In 1994 the Felicia was launched, still budget priced but highly acclaimed by the motoring press (despite the name being described by one journalist as sounding "like a sexual practice with your teeth missing"). Then, in 1998, the Octavia was launched, a breakthrough product that was more than a match for mainstream competitors.

Skoda now found itself in a strange position. Its cars had improved beyond recognition and were now worthy competition for Ford, Vauxhall, Renault and the like. Yet the brand remained hampered by an appalling image, now quite out of step with the reality of the product.

But before this problem found its way to Fallon, there were lessons to be learned from the launch of the Octavia.

Classic planning that backfired – the Octavia launch

It was here that Skoda turned to the rigour of planning. An emotive problem like Skoda's demanded logic and analysis and they turned to an experienced planning consultancy to plot the way forward.

Research showed that the overwhelming problem for Skoda was, quite simply, rejection. 82% of the car buying public were either non-considerers or outright rejectors of the brand. In groups, consumers were categorical that nothing Skoda could say would change their minds.

The planning conclusions were clear. Trying to tackle the ocean of prejudice head on would be impossible and acknowledging this world of cynicism would be counterproductive. Memorably, a document from the time says that trying to convert rejectors would be "like trying to warm up the Pacific Ocean to 75° before you'll go swimming."

The strategy focussed on the 18% of people who displayed varying levels of consideration for Skoda. The idea was to go on the front foot and provide this group with positive messages about Skoda – giving these already susceptible people 'permission to buy.'

In short, by fighting an old war, Skoda risked perpetuating a myth about poor quality. Instead, the way forward for the brand was a targeted, incremental strategy aimed at fishing where the fish were.

A textbook piece of planning, I'm sure you'll agree. But it was flawed. Yet, not because it wasn't logically watertight, nor because it was under-researched.

What went wrong

Creative work was developed for a £10m TV launch. Executionally, the advertising delivered what the strategy had demanded – a front-footed assertion of the rational merits of the Octavia.

Ads focussed on the car's best features and featured the line, "The new Skoda

Octavia. The way things should be." But the 'susceptibles' didn't bite. Sales of the Octavia were extremely disappointing – in the first year only 2569 were sold and the model accounted for a fraction of Skoda's sales.

The strategy Skoda were pursuing had meant that not only had the mass of prejudice against the brand gone unaddressed, but the expected sales gains from targeting 'warmer prospects' had failed to materialise.

Intuitive planning saves the day – the Fabia launch

In 2000 there was another step-change car on the way for Skoda – the Fabia. The new marketing director at Skoda wanted to be sure that he could create a marketing step-change that would avoid this product falling on deaf ears like the last one.

At the end of 1999, Fallon was appointed to answer this brief. Which is where planning comes in again. But our brand of planning had to be very different to that which had gone before. In our minds, planning logic had become the enemy of progress for Skoda (as indeed had listening too intently and uncritically to the consumer).

So where was planning's contribution? We didn't write a proposition that led directly to the creative work. But we did provide a definition of the problem that enabled all of us to look at it with different eyes. In so doing, we provided the creatives with a springboard that helped them to get to an extraordinary creative idea.

Problem definition

Our thinking went like this. Skoda had a great product that was underperforming in the marketplace owing to historical and seemingly unshakeable brand baggage. Yet even those who by quantitative analysis seemed to be warmer to the brand and prepared to consider buying one, were in some way being discouraged from doing so.

This could hardly be for rational reasons, as Skoda now had a winning combination of price and quality that was well accepted by the trade and the motoring press.

It had to be for more emotional reasons. We didn't need to do research to know that choosing a car is for most people a decision that mixes the rational and the emotional. Our contention was that the emotional side of it had more to do with how the purchase would be perceived by others than anything else.

The breakthrough

The stigma surrounding Skoda, we saw, was a shared cultural phenomenon. To target only those who might consider buying one was to ignore the vast mass of their friends, neighbours, colleagues and even children who were likely to ridicule that decision.

The implications were twofold: We needed to change the role for advertising. Even for those who were prepared to consider buying a Skoda, the biggest barrier was irrational prejudice against the brand. The role for advertising therefore had to be to confront that prejudice.

Secondly, the target audience for advertising had to be the British public at large. The aim was to make potential buyers confident that they could choose a Skoda without being laughed at – hence the need to create a general shift in attitudes towards the brand. In other words – talk to those doing the laughing, not just the minority being laughed at.

The creative process

Armed with this new way of looking at the problem, the creatives devised a campaign which explicitly dramatised the prejudice against Skoda. It focussed on people who were made to look stupid by maintaining an outdated view of Skoda.

For the client, this work was at first sight unbuyable. It was one thing to confront prejudice, but by openly showing it were we not running the risk of confirming it?

It was here that planning, and then research, was able to make a further contribution.

First of all, thinking through the fundamental principles of communication allowed us to justify this approach. By saying in essence, "Look at this" and just trying to show that they had changed, Skoda had in the past failed to connect with its audience because the Skoda name had elicited an immediate prejudgement.

Our new approach was to gain a hearing by showing that we know how people view us and then confronting them to reconsider. In essence what we were saying was: "We know what you think of us, but look at this," hence gaining empathy and encouraging consumers to make up their own minds. By acknowledging the prejudice, we argued, we could begin to deflate it.

At last some research

Creative development research tends to gives planners a bad name (especially with creatives). In this case, however, it was essential for proving our hypothesis and giving the client confidence.

As we had hoped, the thinking we had developed through a combination of planning intuition and creative invention was confirmed by consumers. In fact, the idea proved to be a lot cleverer than we had realised.

It became clear that for people to open their minds to Skoda they first needed to have their existing beliefs acknowledged. By 'personifying' their preconceptions in a character in the scripts, we learned that they were able to externalise and laugh at them. In this way, we were able to implicitly 'reposition' the anti-Skoda brigade as being out of touch. The dangers of this approach were defused by doing it through humour.

As one respondent put it: "Skoda used to be the joke. Now the joke is the joke." (Shaw Research, November 1999).

All this portrayed Skoda in a new, confident light and opened the way for consideration of Skoda on a more rational basis now that the emotional stigma had been addressed.

Broadening the campaign

Our media thinking flew in the face of fashionable 'narrowcast' media. In line with our targeting strategy, the limited media budget was allocated to a high profile schedule of TV, posters and landmark press. It was critical that the advertising was as public as possible if we were to shift ingrained cultural perceptions.

We also applied this insight beyond traditional paid-for media. In particular, we saw that for Skoda to win the argument, we needed to take the fight to the people who were laughing the loudest at us – the tabloid press. We therefore appointed a PR agency, Sputnik, with a specific brief of persuading the media that there was a story in talking about Skoda's rebirth.

Afterword

This paper gives a realistic picture of how planning contributed to one of the most successful campaigns of recent years.

The style of planning we adopted was rarely a classic one, and its role veered from strategic to tactical. But without planning, the outcome would have been very different. In particular, the principle of talking to those doing the laughing, not just the minority being laughed at, was a genuine breakthrough.

We would argue that it is in cases like this that the true value of planning as an integral part of the advertising process is demonstrated.

"Because 90% of road accidents are caused by driver error..."

"Daewoo have introduced an important new safety feature in their cars..."

"...a safer driver"

"A free advanced driving course with every car. That'll be the Daewoo"

Campaigns for established product brands
sponsor: Express Train

A car company that saves lives

In 1999, Daewoo Cars was at a crossroads. It needed to develop an innovation to help re-stake its claim as the customer champion of the UK car market. This case demonstrates how Daewoo Cars benefited from a combination of research and insight, which led them to buck market trends and talk about safer drivers, rather than car safety features.

Winners: Megan Thompson, Tom Vick
Agency: DFGW
Creative Directors: Dave Waters, Paul Grubb
Art Director: Claudio Pasqualetti
Copywriter: Eugenia Pacelli
Client: Daewoo
Product: Daewoo Cars IAM Initiative

Introduction

This paper will seek to document account planning's contribution to the development of a new marketing initiative and advertising campaign, that have both proved to be amongst the most innovative that Daewoo Cars has undertaken in its short, but highly successful, history in the UK.

Background

In April 1995, Daewoo Cars launched in the UK amidst a blaze of publicity, offering consumers the chance to deal direct with the manufacturer and to benefit from an exemplary after-sales package.

Although many of the major car manufacturers did not take the newcomer very seriously at first, they started attempting to match Daewoo's offering as soon as they saw market share being eroded.

None of them was in a position to deal direct, due to long-standing franchised dealership arrangements. However, they could attempt to offer their customers a much better after-sales package.

By the middle of 1999, Daewoo was starting to get a little nervous. Key parts of their once-unique package, such as three years' AA cover or three years' free servicing, were now being offered not only by 'bargain basement' rivals such as Proton or Kia, but also by mainstream brands such as Ford and Honda.

Daewoo was also being squeezed by prohibitively large competitive media spends. According to Millward Brown, over 200 different car commercials, featuring 71 different models, were aired in the UK in 1999. Daewoo's share of voice on TV in the same year was just 3% and looked set to fall further in 2000.

If it was to hit extremely ambitious growth targets for 2000, it would need a new initiative to help it to stay one step ahead of the competition. Then it would need to communicate it in an original and impactful way, to ensure maximum, effective share of voice.

Reading the Highway Code – doing the strategic basics

Daewoo had a history of generating consumer goodwill by asking people about their frustrations with the car industry. This had enabled it to introduce numerous small but motivating innovations such as the abolition of delivery charges.

But, by the middle of 1999, we felt that the brand had lost the campaigning edge that had initially enabled it to become the customer champion in this unreconstructed market. So we went back to consumers to see if we could find any emergent hot topics that might enable us to take up arms once again.

Qualitative research was carried out amongst new car buyers, who were non-Daewoo rejectors and who were planning to spend £15,000 or less on their car. We also spoke to existing Daewoo owners in paired depths to gauge whether there were any aspects of the existing buying and owning experience that could provide us with new insights.

Initial results did not seem very promising. People felt that many car companies had dramatically improved their customer service in recent years and they were broadly satisfied with the ownership experience. Virtually everyone agreed that Daewoo's aftersales package was very appealing, but that it was gradually becoming indistinguishable from the offerings of its competitors.

The two big issues of consumer debate at the time were those of UK car prices and safety features.

The initial rumblings of 'rip-off Britain' were appearing in the press in the summer of 1999 and many people were rightly indignant about the disparity in car prices between the UK and mainland Europe.

Unfortunately, it was impossible for Daewoo to standardise its European prices overnight. So it started thinking about car safety.

Virtually every car manufacturer at the time was promoting one or more safety features, whether twin airbags, ABS, side-impact protection systems or anti-submarine seats (whatever they are) and most drivers put these features high on their list of priorities when buying a new car.

However, it was also impossible for us to gain any competitive advantage for Daewoo in this area. Whilst all our cars were well-equipped with twin airbags and ABS, none of them had class-leading safety features. What's more, Volvo had spent the best part of twenty years making its brand synonymous with car safety and we had neither the time nor the budget nor the product to combat this.

The one thing that did strike us about car safety was that it was handled in a very cold, technological, inhuman way and this helped lead us to our strategic breakthrough.

Emergency stop: the key insight

While examining competitive car advertising from the UK and around the world, we hit upon a blindingly simple, yet hugely powerful insight: everyone else talks about safe cars, no-one talks about safe drivers.

The more we thought about this, the more powerful the idea seemed. A car in the wrong hands is a lethal weapon. It can have as many airbags and safety features as you like, but if it's driven by a poor or negligent driver, the benefits of those features are entirely negated.

Evidence from our qualitative research seemed to suggest that some people were driving more recklessly than they used to, as the increased amount of safety equipment in modern cars made them feel safer.

However safe they may have felt, the statistics spoke for themselves. A trawl of government and other road safety websites revealed that over 90% of the 3.6

million road accidents in the UK every year are caused by driver error. Which means that over 90% of the annual 300,000 injuries and 3,500 deaths are potentially preventable.

If we could do our bit to reduce these statistics by making Daewoo drivers safer, we could hopefully help a small number of families avoid the pain of injury or bereavement.

The best way to make Daewoo drivers safer was to offer them free advanced driving lessons with their new car. This would be a great addition to the standard after-sales package, with benefits to Daewoo (increased differentiation and a new cause to champion), the driver (something extra for nothing and the chance of cheaper insurance) and the public at large (fewer accidents).

After further research, it was decided that we should offer these lessons through the Institute of Advanced Motorists (IAM) – the UK's foremost provider of advanced driving tuition. Statistics show that IAM drivers are 50-75% less likely to have an accident than ordinary drivers and it was felt that its name would add credibility to Daewoo's initiative.

This was the idea we were looking for to help Daewoo regain its campaigning edge. We now needed to write an inspirational brief and to produce some fantastic advertising.

Mirror, signal, manoeuvre: the creative briefing

The brief itself was kept as concise as possible, to allow for maximum creative flexibility.

The proposition was simple: Daewoo cares about safer drivers, not just safer cars.

It was supported by a list of facts about UK accident statistics from the DETR, the IAM and the Transport Research Laboratory, as well as by a copy of *Roadcraft* (the Police Drivers Handbook), which teaches the principles of advanced driving and which forms the basis of the IAM's course.

To enable us to produce work which stood out from the crowd, we also wanted the teams working on the brief to understand just how similar our competitors' ads were to each other.

So we cut together a tape showing unbranded clips of car commercials, representing hundreds of millions of pounds of media spend. When asked to name all the brands featured, no-one came close. This underlined the need for our work to look and feel completely different to other car advertising.

The undoubted highlight of the briefing was the afternoon the client and agency team spent in one-on-one tuition with IAM examiners out on the country lanes and motorways of Hertfordshire.

We all learned a huge amount experiencing the tuition for ourselves but, to save our blushes, we're unable to reveal who was deemed good enough to go on to take the IAM test.

It is also worth noting that Daewoo sent people from all of its outlets and from its headquarters on similar training, so they were well-versed in the benefits of advanced driving when talking to potential customers.

Left hand down a bit – creative development research

The original TV concept presented by the agency for the 30-second launch script showed a close-up shot of an airbag which, during the course of the commercial, slowly morphed into the car's driver.

A quick round of creative development research during the pre-production phase revealed that the concept did a great job at communicating the fact that Daewoo was committed to making its drivers safer:

- "They realise there's more to safety than the car."
- "They take safety very seriously."
- "They're a responsible company."

(Source: The Research Practice, October 1999)

However, it lacked somewhat in intrigue, warmth and watchability.

Subsequent development of the idea by the creative team and the commercial's director, Daniel Kleinman, resulted in the opening of the commercial consisting of a series of passing shots along the outside of the Daewoo car in the manner of a public information film. The camera then moves inside the car to reveal the "twist" of the ad – a very quick sequence of the car's airbag morphing into a fat, naked driver.

Whilst a fat, naked bloke was not the first choice of either the client or the BACC, we felt he provided a great counterpoint to the sylphlike, beautiful people, so often seen gracing our competitors' advertising and would therefore provide a strong element of humour and differentiation.

So, as a result of the research and some good lateral thinking, the final film became funnier and more watchable, without losing any of its power to communicate the core message.

But don't just take our word for it.

Ripping up the L-plates: the results

This commercial first ran in January and February 2000, a time during which the press was full of articles pouring scorn on the 'rip-off' prices being charged for cars in the UK.

The negative publicity hit retail sales badly, with first quarter figures for Vauxhall and Renault showing year on year declines of 17% and 49% respectively. (Source: SMMT).

Daewoo managed to buck this trend completely, posting a 36.9% increase on 1999's first quarter performance, despite having no increases in distribution, model range or media spend, (sources: SMMT, Daewoo).

Advertising response directly attributable to TV rose by 18% year on year, whilst our tracking study revealed Daewoo's highest ever claimed advertising awareness score and an Awareness Index three points above Millward Brown's car industry average.

Daewoo's rating on the image dimension "concerned about driver safety" also doubled following the campaign, (sources: Daewoo, Millward Brown)

We also picked up a couple of creative awards (most notably at the BTAA) and helped give birth to a new marketing genre – 'social marketing', as described by Steve Hilton in *The Observer*.

It is also worth noting that, by the middle of the year, at least one other manufacturer had introduced a similar advanced driving programme with another road safety organisation.

Most important of all, by the end of 2000, nearly 7,000 purchasers of new Daewoo cars had asked to be sent details of their nearest IAM test centre and over 650 new Daewoo owners had taken the IAM course. This represents a year on year uplift of over 6% in the total annual number of people taking an IAM test. (Sources: Daewoo, IAM)

Conclusion

Hopefully, this case has demonstrated how a client has benefited from a whole range of creative planning skills and how a combination of research and inspiration was used to produce market-leading insights and innovations, to inspire different creative thinking and to execute effective, award-winning advertising.

If, as a result of this hard work, Daewoo Cars has helped to avert one serious injury or fatality, it (and we) think that's time and money well spent.

HIGHLY COMMENDED
Abbott Mead Vickers BBDO

Campaigns for established product brands
sponsor: Express Train

Meeting the needs of the modern cave person

Planning helped to transform Business Pages from a boring old business-to-business phone directory to an office must-have. The key insight was that Business Pages answers a universal and fundamental human drive to be protected. It's a 'territory marker' which makes us feel secure.

Winners: Clare Roberts, Lucy Edge
Agency: Abbott Mead Vickers BBDO
Creative Director: Peter Souter
Art Director: Simon McQueen
Copywriter: Antonia Clayton
Client: Yell
Product: Business Pages

Identifying the role for advertising

Business Pages is a work thing, not a play thing. A business-to-business phone directory. You use it to find what you need, or want, at work.

Yawning yet? Exactly. Business Pages isn't a blockbusting page-turner.

When you are at work you don't want to spend any time thinking about what you are going to use to find what you need. You are a sleepwalker, reaching for what you know, the one you have always used.

Some print ads had already run, politely explaining what the book did. This wasn't working. Few people had heard of Business Pages, even fewer knew what it actually did, and nobody could be bothered to find out.

It was at the bottom of the pile.

The role for advertising was to get it to the top, and quickly. The difficulty in this task lay in finding a way to wake up the sleepwalkers. And, because our budgets were limited, we had to find a way of waking these sleepwalkers up together, as one united group.

The only problem was, the three groups who were responsible for making decisions about business suppliers could not have been more different:

- PAs and secretaries
- Office managers
- Owner directors

They all worked in small companies, around 20 employees, but that was all they had in common.

The other thing we had to do was to show our sleepwalkers what the book looks like - because there is no guarantee that they would be delivered their own copy. Hmm...a boring subject, diverse targets, and a great big pack shot. What a winning combination!

Our start point - exploring emotions at work

It was clear that the functional 'let's tell them what it is' approach wasn't working.

So, we brainstormed what the emotional benefits of the facts might be. The logic flowed:

- The book lists a comprehensive range of businesses (yawn).
- This comprehensiveness means you know it will have what you are looking for, (slightly less dull).
- Which means you can avoid disaster, prevent a problem becoming a crisis, stop your boss/clients shouting at you, and get on with the next thing, (beginning to sound appealing?)
- So, with Business Pages at your side, you won't get so stressed, you'll feel in control and precious peace of mind will be yours, (pass the phone, I want a slice of that.)

Appealing to diverse targets – the stress proposition

The best thing about this logic was that it sounded as if it could appeal to all of our targets. So, we checked. First of all we looked around us. Yep, advertising people are stressed. And so are our clients. But does everyone suffer from stressful environments?

We trawled the net. There it was. Sites on stress management, working conditions that lead to stress, the negative effects of stress on your ability to work, the psyche of the stressed worker.

According to the Henley Centre "stress is the inescapable catchword of our times." 84% of people claim to suffer from it - and they are as likely to be a clerical worker as a captain of industry.

If Business Pages could help to relieve stress, millions more people could be interested in using it. But, never ones to take anyone else's word for it, we decided to do some qualitative research with our targets.

Our hearts sank. They didn't look like they would have a lot in common. But within minutes they were in violent agreement with one another. Why? One word united them, the word 'work'.

They told us what this word meant to them:
1. Secretaries/PAs:
● "Busy"
● "Too many things to do, not enough time"
● "Stress"
● "Hectic"
2. Office managers:
● "Time consuming"
● "Stress"
● "The more work I do the more I generate"
● "A lot of small things take up so much time"
3. Owner directors:
● "They want the work yesterday"
● "Stressful"
● "Demanding – they want more and more and more these days"

We asked them about the causes of stress. Perhaps different things would stress each target?

No. It was the small things which were the main causes of stress, for the owner directors as well as for the office managers or PAs – the photocopier jamming, running out of headed paper, the coffee machine breaking down, needing a venue in a hurry.

The emerging creative brief

It struck us that these were all things Business Pages could help to sort out.

From this came a working proposition: 'No more stress at work with Business Pages.'

The proposition had the potential to speak to loads of people and it united all our target audiences, irrespective of whether they were a filing clerk or the company director.

We were happy with the broad strategic direction but it still felt a bit flabby. Don't a lot of office tools promise to relieve stress? How should Business Pages manifest itself? What was unique about it? We wanted to delve deeper.

We went back to the people who were most in the habit of using Business Pages. They told us that there was nothing more stressful than being without a copy of their book. They talked about how they regarded it like a bible, a lifeline. They refused to be parted from it; they had to have it there on their desk. It was clearly a precious possession.

We wanted to understand what lay behind this somewhat extreme attitude. Did it speak to something in all of us?

We decided to find a friendly anthropologist. Someone who had spent years observing human behaviour, someone who understood why we do the things we do. We found ourselves sitting in Desmond Morris' Oxford library. Frankly, he was the only anthropologist any of us had ever heard of so he seemed like the best choice!

We explained the behaviour of these loyalists.
He thought it was something to do with one of a number of fundamental human drivers. Behaviours that made the survival of the species more likely during the evolutionary period of the Stone Age – behaviours so successful that they remain with us to this day.

Discussions around the behaviour of our loyalists led us to the conclusion that, for them, Business Pages was answering the drive towards protection.

The drive towards protecting our soft bodies from predators two million years ago made our survival more likely. We lived in caves for security. Today's manifestations of protection are a bit different.

Although we don't have a physical need to protect ourselves from anything more than the elements, we continue to place a great deal of emotional importance in the things which make us feel safe and secure, looked after. They are the blankets and toys we trail around as children. As we grow up these things may become more expensive – houses and cars – but they perform the same function.

Desmond Morris calls them 'territorial markers'. And there is plenty of evidence of territorial markers in the office. Business Pages is also a territorial marker for its loyalists.

Like the security blanket they carried around when they were three years old, they feel safe with a copy of Business Pages on their desk.
Showing this relationship through attachment to the book would signify to people that Business Pages could help to protect them from stress predators – mirroring the loyalists' view of it as an island of safety in a sea of stress.

The final creative brief

We added this protective role to our stress relief proposition: 'Business Pages helps to protect you from stress at work'.

The creative idea

Antonia and Simon, our creative team, took another leap.

They recognised that not only do people who are stressed become very attached to the things which help them, and not only do they become very possessive, having to have the thing there with them, but they actually label these things to make sure no one else takes them.

The creative work

We used customised books to demonstrate modern day territorial markings.
As you can see, there was another benefit in bringing to life the physical presence of the book as a territorial marker – we got ourselves the biggest pack shot ever seen in British advertising.

Our targets would certainly know what to look for when Business Pages was delivered to the office. But would the ads unite our targets?

We decided to do some more groups because we were worried that owner directors might view this personalisation as a bit beneath them.

Not a bit of it. Whilst they didn't admit to this behaviour personally they all 'knew someone' who did. Furthermore, along with the other audiences, they thought it was funny, an acute observation on human nature. According to one owner director from Sheen in London: "That's what you get in the office".

This gave Business Pages a rather more interesting personality, no longer confined to Yawnsville. Nor did we have to worry about each of the ads working only against one target – the target in the ad. The message scrawled by the CEO of a company had the right tone for owner directors but also had secretaries smiling, because it reminded them of their boss.

They wanted to know more of the personalities behind the 'territorial markers'. Simon and Antonia enjoyed creating some new characters, and basing one or two of them on people they knew. (Graham Brown, our vice chairman, was rung by *Marketing Week* who wanted to know if he had been promoted).

The idea that Business Pages was such a big help to someone that they would personalise it elevated its importance. No longer was it just a business-to-business directory, but a must-have in the office.

Media – making the message mean more

We wanted to maximise the communication of the brand proposition by choosing media which people read when they want protection from stress.

Metro was the obvious choice here. What's more stressful than a tube journey – especially one that is taking you to work? It also solved another potentially thorny issue – the small nightmare of finding a publication that our three targets would all read. We were particularly worried about getting through to secretaries - their idea of a read at work was *Hello!*

No job title readership information existed, so our media company, PHD, had to do some research to find out the extent to which our targets were reading *Metro*. They found the highest levels of readership amongst PAs and secretaries at around 40%, and slightly lower levels (around 35%) amongst the other two targets.

We decided to supplement *Metro* with some 23 trade titles for our conscientious directors and managers. These titles are read at work, when our targets are under pressure. The promise of stress protection would have a lot of resonance in this environment.

Summary

Planning found a way to unite three completely different target audiences with the almost universal hook of stress relief.

Planning cemented Business Pages' appeal by tapping into the fundamental human driver of protection, giving the book a much higher place in the hierarchy of needs – a thing with which you feel safe and secure. This made it possible to strike a deep emotional chord with our targets.

Planning worked closely with the creatives to make the ads really involving, relevant and entertaining.

Planning worked with the media agency to find publications that would be read by all targets, and helped to find the places where the 'protection against stress' message would mean the most.

Stone Age thinking has helped Business Pages move from the bottom to the top of the pile, by appealing to the cave person in all of us.

TV:

"A critical part of evening grooming."

"The best a woman can get."

"A close shave"

"Definitely not Gillette"

HIGHLY COMMENDED
Bartle Bogle Hegarty

Campaigns for established product brands
sponsor: Express Train

From the bathroom to the nightclub

This paper is about planning's discovery of a hitherto untapped occasion within the shaving category and how Lynx was able to exploit this territory.
An unusual research technique helped to segment the market in a new way and to discover that shaving can be not just a morning chore but a critical part of the evening grooming ritual.

Winner: Dan Goldstein
Agency: Bartle Bogle Hegarty
Creative Director: Rose Arnold
Art Director: Tony Davidson
Copywriter: Kim Papworth
Client: Lever Fabergé
Product: Lynx Triple Blade Razor

Introduction

Lynx is a brand with a winning communications formula: use Lynx and get the girl. To launch Lynx into the shaving category could have been a straightforward brief - surely the ads would write themselves? A superficial analysis of the problem might have suggested that to assert the Lynx personality in this market place would have automatically made us seem a more a relevant alternative to Gillette.

This paper demonstrates that the Lynx brand wouldn't have been enough in itself to persuade young guys to buy a Lynx Razor. Innovative use of research, a careful evaluation of how to use Lynx values and a real understanding of what men look for in a razor gave us a really successful strategy, helping us develop highly effective and award-winning communication.

Background

Lynx is Europe's leading male deodorant brand and is particularly successful amongst young men[1]. Its success has partly been down to its compelling brand promise of 'helping men seduce women' thanks to its great smelling fragrances. By 1999 Lynx had been so successful, its deodorants business was virtually at saturation point among its target. So together with BBH, Lever Fabergé looked at new markets to extend the brand. We identified shaving as one such opportunity. It was distinctly male, big[2] and had only two significant brands operating within it. There was just one problem, one of these brands was Gillette.

Gillette and the shaving category

Gillette was less a player in the category, more the category itself. It dominates shaving in the UK and around the world[3]. Established in 1901, Gillette has benefited from many generations of use[4] and has maintained leadership by out-innovating[5] and out-spending its competitors[6]. As a result it has taken control of the dialogue within the category, taking for its own all the chief benefits consumers recognise as important in a razor.

It was difficult to see how a competitor brand could find a place in the category to call its own. Even Wilkinson Sword, after decades of marketing, had failed to secure a point of meaningful difference in consumers' eyes. It would be an even bigger challenge for Lynx given it had no history in the category. As a challenger brand, we couldn't attack Gillette head on using their language and category codes; we needed to disrupt. Essentially, we needed to be very different to Gillette and find another way to look at shaving.

The opportunity

We wanted to find a way to attack Gillette that would play to our brand strengths. We started our investigations with the consumer, we wanted to get a real understanding of how men shaved and how they felt about it. We tried an unusual research approach, embarking on a programme of 'Accompanied Shaves'. We recruited friends of friends who were willing to have their personal grooming habits exposed. We went into these young men's bathrooms and closely watched them shaving and asked how they felt about the process. We discovered that not all shaves are equal. The reasons and attitudes towards shaving vary by time of day and occasion.

The morning shave was painful to watch. There was little pleasure in the process, indeed men of all ages loathed it. Their only desire was to "make a boring chore as quick as possible" get on their clothes and go to work, school or college. Men shave in the morning out of a sense of duty, ("I shave for my boss"). Most "do it when [they] are half asleep" and not much care is taken ("I move my hand and the razor does the rest"). Thus the desired benefits from a 'morning razor' are purely functional: speed, closeness (of shave) and safety. This was prime Gillette territory.

An evening shave is very different, particularly when in preparation for a big night out. We observed that this shave was part of a much bigger grooming routine designed to get them in the mood.

A typical evening's grooming routine would begin at around six o'clock after getting home from work or college with a call to mates or to a date to make a plan of action, a quick bite to eat and then another call to tell the mates or the date that you're now ready to get ready.

At seven the clothes for the evening are carefully selected and laid upon the bed and a suitable soundtrack is chosen and played at full blast.

Then at eight there's 'shit, shower, shave' – a shower and shave followed by a strut around the bedroom whilst moisturising and deodorising and a quick preen of the hair in the mirror.

At nine thirty, wallet checked, taxi booked. One more phone call to check arrangements. One more glance in the mirror rewarding yourself with a well rehearsed 'OK, let's get 'em' look of admiration. And then leave.

The key learnings we took from this research were:
● Evening 'grooming' is all about giving you the self-confidence to go out on the pull – "feeling up for it and with the look to get it".
● It was an exciting process.
● Shaving is central to this ritual. "The phrase is 'shit, shower, shave' not 'shit, shower, hair wash'".[7]

Far from being wished away, shaving here was viewed as a critical part of getting ready to go out. A quantitative check confirmed that an evening shave was an experience that most men would be able to relate to. We found that 17% of shaving occasions are in the evening and this figure was proportionately higher amongst younger men[8]. If this figure was directly translated into volume we would be four times the size of Wilkinson Sword's best selling razor. We believed that the evening occasion held the potential for a more engaging take on what shaving could be about for young guys.

Can Lynx own evening shaves?

The next piece of research helped us to understand whether Lynx could own the evening shave opportunity. We looked at a number of shaving promises - covering close, smooth, refreshing, hassle-free and creative – and allowed respondents to construct their ideal evening shave. We discovered that the perfect shave for this occasion was all about feeling good and looking good, confirming what we had seen during the 'accompanied shaves.'

We went on to look at which brand could own these values. We learnt that whilst young men had a huge trust in and respect for Gillette's technology, the brand itself held little emotional appeal for them. Gillette's representation of 'masculine achievement' was outdated and irrelevant to them. Gillette represented the 'clean cut, chisel-jawed' face of the male Adonis. He is "the best a man can get", but "he's too perfect". Gillette was seen as a big corporate American brand that was "good but not cool". The opposite was true for Lynx. Lynx held strong appeal for younger men exactly because it understood them and how it really felt to be 'a man'. When the two brands were compared to one another the differences between them were magnified in consumers minds. According to research by 2cv, Lynx was seen as modern, social, likeable and younger, while Gillette was viewed as out-of-date, professional, inaccessible and older.

Gillette's values were associated with performance and achievement, perfect for the functional requirements of a morning shave. The evening shave with its upbeat vibe and 'social motives' played directly into Lynx's values. So, when asked which brand fits best in an evening occasion, the answer was unequivocally Lynx and definitely not Gillette – "yuppies and fighter pilots do not feel up for it"[9].

The consumer insight

Our insight was therefore incredibly simple: 'Shaving is a critical part of the grooming process for young men getting ready to go out'.

The product insight

During the groups we realised the importance of convincing people that we had a credible product. This was particularly important to the younger, less confident guys who required reassurance that the Lynx Razor would shave brilliantly as well as being 'cooler' than Gillette. All our research had suggested that 'a close shave' was the criteria by which the performance of a razor was judged. The challenge was to demonstrate this functional performance in a Lynxy way rather than using Gillette-like product stories.

Our insight came from within the account team. Our rugby playing account director claimed that he would shave after a match rather than before. He used his stubble in the scrum to irritate his opponent's faces 'like sandpaper', shaving only after a game as 'the wife' didn't appreciate the same treatment. 'A close shave' could equal 'closer to women'. We tested this hypothesis through interviews with both men and women. We found that whilst men believed a close shave was important when smooching (or trying to), women claimed that it was indeed smooth skin that they most appreciated from their shaved men. The fact that the Lynx Razor had three blades gave them ample reassurance that the product was up to the job. With this seduction spin, the category generic of 'closeness' was a product insight that could both reassure and engage.

Launch communications strategy

Our communications strategy for the Lynx Razor launch was now in place:
- Exploit the evening shave.
- Own for Lynx via seduction.
- Reassure on product delivery by promising closeness (support with three blades).

The brief and briefing

Our brief and briefing were all about how we were going to own the evening shave for Lynx.

Our creative proposition summed up what Lynx was going to bring to the category. It was a deliberate subversion of Gillette's own property: "The new Lynx Razor is the best a woman can get."

This proposition set the communications agenda on several levels:
- It put the emphasis of a Lynx shave on being attractive to women.
- It was a stake in the ground as to our clear opposition to Gillette and how it talked about shaving.
- Its tone gave permission to the creative team to be funny and irreverent.
- It implied the same product performance as the market leader.

We then explained how this should take shape: We described to the creative team the excitement of an evening shave – getting men psyched up and ready to go out and pull. We brought the atmosphere and feelings of this occasion to life, sharing our notes from the accompanied sessions and quoting the guys we had observed.

The closeness of the Lynx shave was the key product benefit we wished to get across. Without a high performance razor, there would be no reason to feel confident and 'up for it', given girls' attraction to smooth-shaved men.

Steering away from Gillette

To develop an understanding of Gillette's communication codes we worked together with a semiotician to study 15 years worth of Gillette advertising. We talked the creative team through our observations and asked for the work to be as different from Gillette in every way possible.

The Gillette communication codes:
- A ready made 'wife'
- All American
- Inaccessible hunk – he's perfect, infallible
- Penthouse suite, huge family house or mansion
- Tell us how great the razor is
- Satisfied with just his shave
- The product has a name - Mach 3
- Corporate signature tune
- Jet plane, fire engines, offices
- 'Out of date' masculine heroes
- Serious

The idea

The creative idea was immediately liked by the brand team. At its heart the ad, called *Strike*, is a demonstration of the product insight of 'closeness' in the context of an evening's preparation to go out. Our hero then meets his date and attempts to impress her by lighting a match against his chin. Of course, the Lynx shave is so effective that he fails miserably. Fortunately his companion is able to oblige.

Our discussion during the briefing regarding Gillette communication codes was used very skilfully by the creative team to develop the script further in an attempt to distance ourselves wholeheartedly from Gillette territory.

Lynx anti-Gillette communication codes included:
- Young, free and single
- Turkish (Eastern in appearance)
- He is fallible. His red underpants make him vulnerable
- Bedsit (untidy)
- He treats the razor as if it's precious
- Satisfied with his whole appearance
- The process has a name - 3 Blade Shave
- Dodgy Turkish techno tune (written by the creative team)
- Moped

- Retro styling
- Funny

Having seen the finished film it is difficult to imagine 'Lynx Shaving' taking on any other form. The evening occasion territory had helped to justify Lynx's presence in the category and represented a real uncharted insight into how young guys use a razor. Tonally it felt very un-Gillette – cool, insightful and extremely funny!

Results

Strike was extraordinarily successful in meeting our objectives:

- "As in previous Lynx communication the brand is demonstrating its understanding of young guys: it is in touch" (Source: Flamingo Finished Film Research July 2000)
- *Strike* achieved a Millward Brown Preview Effectiveness index of 119. It concluded: "*Strike* is highly enjoyable and very impactful. The second highest score for a launch ad we have ever seen. Even though it does not follow the traditional 'toys for boys' approach it does communicate the rational product benefit". 84% took that 'The Lynx razor gives a 'close shave'' spontaneously from the communication. (Source: Millward Brown: *Strike* Preview-Test Debrief)
- Spontaneous Awareness of the new razor reached 49% amongst 16-24 year old men. (Source Millward Brown Tracking Dip)
- The trade was so enthusiastic about the Lynx proposition that we achieved 90% distribution in just five weeks with the campaign supported heavily in store. (Source: Lever Fabergé)
- Lynx value share of the UK razors and blades market during the second week of communication reached 9.8% in multiples (higher than any other brand or shaving system bar Gillette's Mach 3). The hardware communication had a halo effect on other products in the shaving range; Lynx value share of the shaving software market reached 6.9% (the second highest brand share after Gillette) over the same period. (Source: Fasttabs)

Strike has also received critical acclaim, including a Silver Arrow at the British Television Advertising Awards. The Daily Telegraph commented: "Compare these ads – fresh relevant and engaging – with the dull clichéd fare Gillette serves up. Unless it does something for younger shavers Gillette is going to lose this market".

Conclusions

Lots has been written about the theory of how you go about challenging a brand leader. This is a story about how you do it in practice. We started out with a great brand, but we realised that it wasn't just enough to rely on our distinctive brand values alone. Planning was instrumental in identifying a usage occasion that Lynx could own, developing a motivating product story and making sure that all this was reflected in our advertising.

In particular, by understanding the role that evening shaving has in young men's lives, we were able to create a completely fresh perspective on the whole process, and in turn, take shaving out of the bathroom and into the nightclub.

[1] Lynx value share of the UK male deodorants category was over 40% in 1999 and Lynx value share of both male and female deodorants was 17% in the UK and 11% in Europe (source: Fasttabs). 35% of all men use Lynx Deodorant in the UK and 66% of 15-24 year olds use Lynx most often (source: TGI 1999).

[2] The shaving category (both razors & blades and shaving software) was worth £260m in the UK (source: Fasttabs) and $2.8bn in Europe in 1999 (source: Euromonitor).

[3] Gillette's value share of the shaving category was 70% in the UK in 1999 (source: Fasttabs). The then newly launched Mach 3 razor had by the end of 1999 taken over 20% value share of the $8bn global shaving category (source: Euromonitor).

[4] 40% of all men in the UK use a Gillette razor most often when shaving (source: TGI 1999).

[5] The Mach3 reputedly had a development cost of $1bn (source: Gillette Annual Report 1999).

[6] Between 1996-99 Gillette's advertising spend in the UK was £37m versus Wilkinson Swords' £8.5m (source: MMS).

[7] Source: BBH research - all quotes.

[8] Source: Taylor Nelson ETCD December 1999, a European panel of men's personal care habits collected in diaries.

[9] Source: 2cv and Firefish research.

HIGHLY COMMENDED
BMP DDB

Campaigns for established product brands
sponsor; Express Train

How mums learned to Brooke Bond with their kids

This paper tells the story of how, in order to make sure that children were picking up the tea habit, planning positioned tea in a competitive set of school runs and bedtime stories: opportunities to give mums a chance to bond with their kids. Planning understood how tea is able to help bridge the generational divide because it takes time to drink and, like adults, kids chat when they drink it.

Winner: James Hillhouse
Agency: BMP DDB
Creative Director: Larry Barker
Art Director: Paul Angus
Copywriter: Ted Heath
Client: Van den Bergh Foods
Product: PG Tips

Introduction

It is a truth universally acknowledged by marketing managers that kids under the age of twelve haven't picked up the tea habit as their parents once did. This paper tells the story of how planning attempted to reverse this trend.

The lost art of tea drinking

BMP's econometric wing, DDB Matrix, was commissioned to undertake a project investigating the decline in tea consumption[1]. In doing so it uncovered a long-term generational effect contributing to this decline. Put simply, children were not picking up the tea habit. This problem was being exacerbated by the fact that soft drinks were outspending tea by four to one[2]. PG Tips, as the market leader in the tea category, decided to start reversing this trend.

NPD not an option

Previous research undertaken by PG Tips had suggested that taking on soft drinks would mean investing in NPD. But the kind of product this would lead to would be closer to soft drinks than to tea. It would not be a guarantee that children would switch to proper tea when they were older. The challenge was to make kids keen on tea as it currently stood.

Kids may not be the target

Taking on soft drinks to make tea appealing to disinterested kids felt like a huge task, maybe an impossible one. To find out just how big the problem was, we grabbed space on a Unilever piece of quantitative research[3]. Fortunately reports of tea's demise had been greatly exaggerated. Seven out of ten kids actually did drink tea; the problem was that only two out of ten did so on a daily basis. So the challenge wasn't to get kids to start drinking tea, it was to transform them from tea dabblers into tea junkies.

But the research also told us that mums have more influence over the drinks their kids had at home than we'd imagined, much more so than with snacks and cereals. In other words our initial hypothesis was wrong. What we had to do was to get mums to offer tea to their kids rather than for the kids to ask for it themselves. This felt like a more manageable task. And so our target aged by about twenty-five years.

National health

At the time that we were developing this strategy, there was a lot of press coverage about the scientific investigations in to tea's health benefits. Tea contained antioxidants[4] and could be good for you. This seemed like a story to tell mums to get their kids drinking more tea. A health message would have an obvious benefit for mums – 'you're doing your job properly, and because of this your kids will be healthy'. The mums we spoke to in the agency confirmed that their main worry in giving soft drinks was that they would rot their nippers' teeth. Everyone seemed pretty content that this could be our strategy. To make sure we weren't congratulating ourselves prematurely we decided to check what some non-advertising mums thought . We set up some groups.

To be honest there was a nagging doubt at the back of my mind. I wasn't too convinced that people saw tea as a healthy drink, especially vigilant mums keeping an eye on what their kids drank, but I needed to check whether this was a valid concern or just excessive paranoia.

Health catches a cold

I made a bee-line for Purley to talk to some mums. Almost immediately the health strategy fell apart. Taking me under their motherly wing they explained that the amounts of tannin tea contained made it as much of a teeth rotter as soft drinks[5].And the thought that a caffeine-based drink[6] could be considered in the same set of drinks as water and fruit juices was laughable. Especially when their kids drank it with a bucketload of sugar.

The generation game

As the groups went on, it was obvious that the sociability thought that was more relevant to my mind was more relevant to theirs as well. It transpired that there was something of a generational divide developing between mums and their kids. During the warm-up we had chatted about their relationships with their kids, and to a (wo)man, they'd all bemoaned two things:
1. "I never see my kids. As soon as they get home they're off upstairs."
2. "I haven't got a clue what they're in to. Alan Shearer I know, but God knows about Nintendo."

These mums didn't know their Banjo the Bear from their TipTup the Turtle[7], and they weren't getting the opportunity to put this right.

The more we talked, the clearer it became that this was largely because the occasion when they traditionally spent some 'quality time' with their children – when they got back from school – was being snatched away from them. Instead of chatting with mum, kids were running off to listen to music or zombifying themselves in front of TVs or Playstations in their rooms. Mums were suffering the tweenage backlash. What made this worse was that unlike many other occasions when you spent time with your kid – the school run, the bedtime book etc. – having a chat here wasn't just the by-product of doing something else, it was the whole reason for sitting down in the first place. So, when mums did get the chance to talk to their kids they weren't chatting, they were being updated on the day at school. As a result they were becoming world experts on Roman drainage systems, but weren't finding out a great deal about their children.

To be fair the mums admitted this wasn't entirely their kids' fault. Because school runs and bedtime stories were times when they were 'playing mum', they acted accordingly: 'Because I don't see the boys so much, I feel like I should be checking up on school things, because that's what mums do.'

What they were looking for was something that would allow them to step outside this responsibility, and let them talk to their kid as a friend instead of as 'a mum'.

In the adult world tea traditionally played a key role in bringing people together. The question was, could it do the same thing between adults and children? Could tea be positioned in a competitive set of school runs and bedtime stories rather than juices and pop?

Taking on the school run

It seemed more sensible for tea to be competing here than against soft drinks. Juices and pop were drinks that because they were so quick to make and consume, were allowing kids to run off as soon as they got through the door. They were actually widening the generational divide rather than bridging it. Tea, on the other hand, was a drink that took time both to make and drink and had to be savoured.

But more importantly, it became apparent that kids behaved differently when they drank tea. Just as their first alcoholic drink will be in ten years time, a drink of tea represented a tentative step into the adult world. And once there, they behaved like proper adults do – they had a chinwag.

One mum put it this way: "My girl went for tea to a friend's and had a cup (of tea). When she came back she was all chatty and grown up. She reckoned she was a proper grown up 'cause she'd had a cup of tea and I guess she behaved that way. We had a proper natter." This statement was met with vigorous nods from virtually all the mums – when you gave your kid tea, they'd chat.

We therefore had the opportunity to create a halfway point between mum and kid, where the kids were willing to chat and the mums were willing to listen. A place where mums would be able to step out of their parental role and find out stuff about their kid that they normally wouldn't have the foggiest about. It was a more sociable, liquid equivalent of a bedtime book. People were leaving the groups saying that when they got home they were going to have a cuppa and a chat with their kids. It looked like we were on to a winner.

A spoonful of sugar

The danger with this sort of message was that it could produce the kind of sentimental advertising that would have people reaching for the sick bucket rather than the kettle. Luckily PG Tips has an irreverent, cheeky tone of voice[8]. Our communications needed to employ this.

The brief

- Target: mums with young kids who find that they don't spend as much time with their kids as they'd like to.
- Message: PG Tips will help you bond with your kids.
- Support: because it takes time to make and drink, because it's calming and they see it as quite adult, it'll slow them down. This may well lead to getting to know your kids better. In the process you'll find out what's important to them, from CITV to what's cool at school.
- Tone: warm, but cheeky. Avoid Werther's Original nausea-inducing sentiments.

In addition, I chatted with my nephew and niece and their mates. They helped me put together a list of things they were into, from Pokémon to Pogs. Because of this I am still able to tell you that Horsea, a water-based Pokémon, is number 116 and will eventually evolve into Seadra.

This list of what kids liked was given to the bemused creative teams.

The work

The work produced by Ted Heath and Paul Angus was bang on the money. The creative consisted of two mugs together, one belonging to the mum, one belonging to their kid. The Mum's mug had a message on it describing the benefit she'd get from sitting down with her kids. The endline was a suitably informal 'share a cuppa with the kids'.

Creative development

We only needed two executions, but Ted and Paul got on enough of a roll to produce five. We put them into creative development research.

It quickly became clear that we needed to draw a line between stuff mums wanted to find out and stuff they'd rather not know about. So the execution 'Find out who's the champion spitter of 2B' was nasty behaviour and best not dwelt on. Whereas 'Find out the latest word for willy', although a little naughty, was what kids said. The research also suggested that the executions that worked best were gender specific. When we attempted to straddle both worlds, we ended up being vague rather than insightful. The two executions therefore ended up being – 'Learn the latest word for willy' (for the boys) and 'find out who this week's best ever, ever friend is' (for the girls).

Teatime reading

The strategy dictated where the ads should be placed. We wanted mums to see them when they were having a cuppa and were in a relaxed state of mind, hopefully feeling a little sentimental about their children (as opposed to wanting to throttle them). Ideally, when their kid had just run off somewhere. Initiative Media drew up a plan that placed the executions in 'tea break' magazines (to call them coffee break would be heresy). It was *Take a break, Chat,* and *Bella* all the way.

Conclusion

This paper has attempted to demonstrate how planning turned a long-term generational decay and a seeming need for kids to pick up the tea habit into an opportunity for mums to step out of their parental role for a minute and bridge the generational divide with their kids. The key to doing this was to position tea in a competitive set of school runs and bedtime stories rather than fruit juices and pop.

[1] The market has declined by around a quarter since 1985, according to AC Nielsen.
[2] Based on 2000 MMS figures.
[3] The 'Kid and Kin' study
[4] Antioxidants are vitamins, minerals or enzymes that help to protect the body from the formation of free radicals. Free radicals are atoms that can cause damage to cells, impairing the immune system and contributing to conditions such as the ageing process and cancer.
[5] The tannin contains the tea's antioxidants.
[6] Tea does contain caffeine, but half the amount contained by coffee.
[7] Characters from the computer game *Diddy Kong Racing*.
[8] The *chimps* being the classic embodiment of this.

New brands or
new advertisers

The APG Creative Planning Awards

Category Sponsor

Hall & Partners is delighted to sponsor the APG Awards this year. We were particularly keen to sponsor the 'new brands and new advertisers' category as it is often when clients have something new to say that they break away from their traditional research methods and look for a research partner who can offer a new and different approach to brand and advertising research. Our congratulations to all the prize winners in this category, and particularly to Richard Warren for the Imperial War Museum work – a challenging and inspiring brief.

Hall & Partners Europe
14-19 Great Chapel Street, London W1F 8FN
Telephone: 020 7534 4500   www.hall-and-partners.com

Cinema:

"Have you ever wondered what Man could achieve when he really sets his mind on it?"

"What he could build and plan, how he could inspire others to do things they never dreamed they could do?"

"If you've ever wondered what Man is truly capable of, now's your chance to find out."

GOLD
Delaney Lund Knox Warren

New brands or new advertisers
sponsor: Hall & Partners Europe

The Holocaust: You need to know

With a limited budget and tough competition, advertising had to generate interest and media coverage for the Imperial War Museum's Holocaust Exhibition, but without resorting to a sensational approach. Planning identified a target audience that likes to have its thinking challenged, and consequently a new way of looking at the Holocaust: as an extraordinary human achievement.

Winner: Richard Warren
Agency: Delaney Lund Knox Warren
Creative Directors: Gary Betts, Malcolm Green
Art Director: Gary Betts
Copywriter: Malcolm Green
Client: Imperial War Musem
Product: Holocaust Exhibition

123

Introduction

Writing about the Holocaust is an uncomfortable experience. Writing about advertising the Holocaust is an even more uncomfortable experience. But writing about advertising the Holocaust in order to enter some awards that celebrate 'the best that account planning can offer' feels beyond the realms of good taste.

However, we plead a fair hearing. We advertised the Imperial War Museum's Holocaust Exhibition because we believe that people need to go because they need to know. We are writing this paper because we continue to believe people need to know. We are also writing it because it demonstrates the power of planning in the advertising process. By planning, we mean the thinking that comes before the making.

Planning achievement

This is a story of a leap that was made in the thinking process - a leap that provided a powerful platform for persuasive advertising. As with most leaps of thought, it was achieved by coming at a subject from a different angle. Also, as with most leaps of thought, it was achieved by a team of people not by an individual.

Background

Four years in the making, the Holocaust Exhibition is a permanent exhibition developed by and housed at The Imperial War Museum (IWM). Described as "a narrative history in 27 chapters", it uses historical material to tell the story of the Nazis' persecution of the Jews and other groups before and during the Second World War. The 1200 square metre historical display brings to this country for the first time rare and important artefacts, some of them from former concentration and extermination camp museums in Germany, Poland and Ukraine. For example, a death cart from a Warsaw ghetto, a medical table on which experiments were carried out, last letters written by victims, and shoes of those imprisoned at concentration camps.

The exhibition attempts to bring some understanding to what happened and why. In his foreword to the exhibition, Robert Crawford, the museum's director-general says: "The Holocaust Exhibition documents one of the darkest chapters in the history of western civilisation. I urge you to see this exhibition and ponder its deeper meanings and the lessons it offers for the future."

Fighting in a highly competitive market

The IWM receives funds for its development programme from the Government, corporate sponsors and individual donations. A key part of its income is also made up of admission charges.

Opened by the Queen on Tuesday 6 June 2000, the Holocaust Exhibition was the Imperial War Museum's millennium event. Making it tougher for the IWM, there were three other new London attractions emerging at the same time, all competing for people's time and money: the Dome, the London Eye and the Tate Modern. They were big, they were high profile and they were supported by much higher marketing budgets.

The client brief

In the face of this stiff competition, the IWM set aside a budget of £150k to market the Exhibition, with advertising destined to play a lead role. The Museum's stated objective was: 'To bring in visitors to the Holocaust Exhibition in a responsible way'.

The IWM set itself a target of 50,000 visitors in the first year, over and above schools. To drive traffic from day one, momentum needed to be built around the launch. Any advertising needed to stimulate and support a PR programme. Our job was to use advertising to create interest in the Exhibition in a responsible way.

The brief recognised the fine line that needed to be trodden: "It is a very delicate area. Any notions of 'marketing the Holocaust' need to be avoided" (Suzanne Bardgett, project director). With a limited budget, and the need to create interest, there was an especial need for advertising to grab attention, but it had to avoid a sensational or shocking approach for fear of scaring off potential visitors, causing adverse PR, and upsetting or offending various interested parties. We would need to work closely with the Holocaust Exhibition's advisory group, the members of which include distinguished historians, Jewish religious leaders and Holocaust survivors.

The target

A budget of £150k calls for precision targeting. Initial discussions with the IWM suggested there were certain groups who would get to know about the Exhibition and would naturally feel impelled to go. They included IWM repeat visitors, the Jewish community and those in education. We needed to focus on the second tier: those who were most likely to go if we could generate sufficient interest.

The IWM's data showed that 35% of adults visit museums every year[1]. They are more likely to be educated and from higher socio-economic classes. The IWM describes them as "intellectually engaged and emotionally responsive": people who have a natural urge to educate themselves (and their children); they are socially concerned and politically active - the 'Knowledge Hungry.'

A quick re-cap

The bits of the jigsaw were fitting into place:
● We had a clear task: to stimulate interest, responsibly.

125

- We had identified our target as the 'Knowledge Hungry'.
- We needed to grab attention in a highly competitive market and with a limited budget; ideally, advertising needed to generate PR in and of itself .
- But we needed to avoid sensationalism and scare tactics for fear of frightening off potential visitors, causing adverse PR and upsetting interest groups.

So what to do and what to say?

A new way of looking at the Holocaust

We returned to our target - the 'Knowledge Hungry.' Whilst they are well educated and keen to absorb as much new knowledge as possible, what they relish is new insights and thoughts, different points of view. They are stimulated by debate and argument. In fact, the calibre and originality of their points of view and perspectives is a crucial determinant of their self-worth.

It is this thirst for new and original insight that underlies the popularity, amongst this group, of the editorial and op-ed pages of broadsheet newspapers, magazines such as *The Spectator, New Statesman* and *Prospect*, and, in particular, revisionist history and biography.

For this target, there was a certain familiarity, dare we say fatigue, with the Holocaust. They would probably have a firm knowledge of the Second World War having studied it at school; they would have seen recent Holocaust films like *Schindler's List* and *Life is Beautiful*. The images and themes of the textbooks and films can be seen and read on Holocaust websites that we visited, of which there are over one million: You cannot escape 'horror', 'death', 'suffering', 'tragedy', 'hatred', 'persecution', 'murder on a massive scale'. The overriding theme of the Holocaust is one of human atrocity. Simply to replay this theme back to the target would offer no new insight and would fail to create sufficient interest. Equally, the lack of a new point of view, by definition, would be unlikely to generate PR.

We had to find a new way of looking at the Holocaust that would stimulate interest.

One of the truly frightening things about the Holocaust is how planned and systematic the slaughter was, and how ruthlessly and efficiently it was carried out. Looking at it from a different angle, to surgically remove an entire race together with the necessary attendant recasting of social, cultural and historical truth; and to incarcerate and successfully kill six million people was a quite extraordinary feat of humankind. In other words, the Holocaust can be looked upon as an act of extraordinary human achievement as opposed to extraordinary human atrocity.

It is a new way of looking at a familiar subject that satisfies our target's desire for fresh perspectives. It is a shift in thinking that forces reappraisal, somehow making the event seem even more unpalatable and frightening. And human achievement is exactly what exhibitions celebrate.

The creative brief and media strategy

The heart of the creative brief was as follows.

The advertising objective: 'To stimulate responsible debate about the Holocaust.'

The advertising proposition: 'Visit The Holocaust Exhibition to witness another extraordinary achievement of Man.'

The media strategy was informed by three elements: the budget; what media our target interacted with; and how we could engage the target in order to stimulate a responsible debate.

● The budget ensured we concentrated solely in the London area.
● Possible media options were TV, press, outdoor and cinema.
● We reduced these options to cinema and cross tracks – we wanted to capture the audience in a public environment, when they had time to contemplate the message: 'Meditation Media'.

An art-house package was bought at venues such as Hampstead, Clapham and Camden to instigate debate amongst a captive audience. The sort of films the advertising would run in were *Nurse Betty, The Luzhin Defence, Snatch, High Fidelity* and *Long Walk to Freedom*. Cross tracks were weighted to areas such as Hampstead, Chiswick, Clapham and Wimbledon.

The creative work

The creative work takes the proposition on and plays with it to full effect. Accompanied by bright and jaunty music we are introduced to what we believe to be one of the pyramids in Egypt. The voice-over asks: "Have you ever wondered what man could achieve when he really sets his mind on it?" (In order to achieve an appropriately upbeat tone, the voice-over artist was not told what the ad was for). As the camera pulls slowly back, the narrator continues: "...what he could build...and plan...how he could inspire others to do things they never dreamed they could do..."

By this time, the audience is becoming aware that this is not one of the pyramids. It could be a building, perhaps a church.

As the narrator says, "If you've ever wondered what Man is truly capable of...now's your chance to find out," the camera now pulls out to its widest shot. The 'pyramid' is in fact the roof of the entrance gate to Auschwitz. The music becomes hollow before being replaced with the unmistakable voice of Adolf Hitler. A title appears. It reads: 'The Holocaust Exhibition. You need to know.'

The approach is disarmingly simple. The effect is chilling.

The film uses no horrific footage, no scenes of death or torture. No shots of

127

Nazis or their victims. The jolt the audience receives when the twist is revealed is haunting.

The theme of man's achievement is continued in the print work.

It is a creative solution that seeks to maximise response without inviting hostility or opposition from any interest group. It is a creative solution that maximises the power of the original thought.

Results

Believing that excellent creative work is also effective creative work, there are two bits of evidence of success that we want to leave you with:

● The advertising stimulated extensive PR, both at a national and international level, including *The Wall Street Journal*. The greatest achievement was a ten minute feature on *Newsnight*; the full commercial was played, and discussion focussed on the advertising as much as the Exhibition. It was ideal programming for our target: prime time debate.

● From day one, traffic has been way above target, achieving an average of one thousand visitors a day.

What planning achieved

Planning did the basics in providing clear parameters for advertising development and a clear role for advertising: To stimulate responsible debate. But, better than that, by making a leap, planning got to a powerful core thought: The Holocaust was a phenomenal human achievement not just an horrific human atrocity. It was a thought that was maximised in the creative process to produce chillingly persuasive advertising. As Naomi Grinn said on *Newsnight*: "It's simple, clever...and sends a shiver down my spine"

[1] Source: IWM/MGC Research 1999

Press:

Stirring up press coverage....

Poster:

SILVER
Bartle Bogle Hegarty

New brands or new advertisers
sponsor: Hall & Partners Europe

Betting on-line with notoriety

The Paddy Power story tells how planning was adapted to a modern world that needs results faster. Paddy Power, Ireland's leading bookmaker, introduced itself to the UK population with a deliberately notorious campaign born out of the simple observation that a new generation of gamblers uses betting to make everyday life more interesting.

Winners: Jonathan Shaw, Dylan Williams
Agency: Bartle Bogle Hegarty
Creative Director: Russell Ramsay
Art Director: Rik Brown
Copywriter: Jon Fox
Client: Paddy Power
Product: Online Betting

Introduction

This was going to be presented as a pure and simple dot.com success story. After all, there aren't many around these days. But it's not really about all that. The planning challenges in this instance were not really unique to dot.com accounts. In truth, the planner's struggle on accounts like Paddy Power simply stirred deep suspicions we'd held about the discipline for a while. Namely:

- Are we slowing things up in a world that wants things quicker ?
- Are the ads getting worse now that planning has got big ?

Now we've been ducking these suspicions for some time now. We block our ears when we hear that three times as much time is donated to strategy development as to creative development. We shut our eyes when someone plays a D&AD reel alongside an IPA Effectiveness one. We never let it bother us. We just get the planning award, get pissed and get the pay rise.

Unfortunately we couldn't in this instance. The client wouldn't let us. Nor would our creative director. They both wanted great work and they both wanted it super quick and they both wanted to know what planning was going to do to help.

So this story isn't really about dot.coms. It's about how we addressed our suspicions and reassured ourselves that planning can still be useful. It's about how we evolved the planning process and the relationship between planner and creative team. And it's about the specific planning contribution within the new process. About foresight, insight, benefits and the power of fame.

And just to spice things up – I've got a tenner it gets further than the Lynx paper.

The challenge

Paddy Power is Ireland's biggest bookmaker. Formed through merger and acquisition, it has grown through a mixture of punter-friendly bets, strong bricks and mortar presence and great service. It's a pretty powerful package - if you're in Ireland.

When they came to us with a plan to launch as a dot.com in the UK the challenge was daunting. How could we find space for an unknown Irish brand in a UK market dominated by a few 'old guard' players ? How could we take a betting service on-line and rapidly drive site traffic ? This wasn't just a 'new brand' job. It was a 'new brand and new channel' job.

Moreover on a broader level we faced the more fundamental challenge. What could we do to planning to ensure it would help get better creative work, quicker? It was this that we turned to first.

From proposition-led to task-based planning

However we dress it up, planning remains an essentially linear, sequential process.

First we agree objectives, then we tailor strategy which we summarise with a proposition, and then we hand over to a creative team to execute. This takes time. In most instances, good planners will get to the right strategic territory quite quickly, but then slow up when attempting to summarise their thinking with a pithy Byronesque sentence. Moreover, according to our creative directors, this level of précis is not always necessary. There is an emergent generation of creative teams who are less driven by propositions. Instead they like to get involved earlier in the process, working within a well defined area, rather than with a well crafted sentence. They get better work out that way.

On the back of these observations we agreed up front to dispense with the linear approach and tried to be more fluid and concurrent. We dropped the proposition-led brief and instead adopted a task-based approach.

This felt right. We could fast track to creative development without skimping on strategic guidance – making the process quicker. And the teams felt more comfortable and got involved for longer – increasing the chances of better work.

With a new path in place we set out on our next step. We had to identify an area within which to couch the brand's benefit, and then share it with the creative team early.

Identifying the market opportunity

The first thing that struck us when we surveyed the UK betting landscape was how similarly all the brands behaved. Everyone concentrated on the most direct, rational betting benefit – it could make you rich. The orthodoxy of gambling advertising said that all you need to do is to dangle the prospects of big winnings in front of the consumer.

All this rational communication was fundamentally about stimulating current betters to bet more. All eyes were on the present. No one was looking at the market's future.

Betting is one of those things that will inevitably get shaken up by new technologies. As more people get connected, betting's constituency will broaden massively – expanding out from downmarket older males to include younger, wealthier males and females. But how would this change things?

It struck us that Las Vegas was a microcosm for how the betting industry as a whole was changing. Originally Vegas had just been about money. And how the betting hardcore could clean it. But it had evolved into an entertainment destination for a far wider market. Its focus had moved from cash to enjoyment, from the rational to the emotional.

Defining a relevant benefit

Your typical bloke down the bookies is primarily driven by rational motives. 'New

School' gamblers aren't. These people are driven more by emotional motives - by the pursuit of enjoyment.

Datamonitor's predictions of future betting trends reflected this. The emphasis on traditional betting topics (horses, dogs etc) will ease off as people start gambling on a much wider variety of things - from other sports and politics, to the Oscars and *Big Brother*. The future will be less about obsessing over 'the form'; it will be more about having a playful bet on a wider variety of stuff.

That's because gambling will become a leisure pursuit: no longer about the probability of riches, but instead driven by the promise of a heightened experience. A quick hit of fun. A bit of a laugh. We saw that to be relevant to the betting consumers of the future Paddy Power needed to be about fun and enjoyment.

Credibility from the inside out

We were wary about creating an advertising myth around Paddy Power that the company couldn't live up to. We had to ask if Paddy Power could credibly couch its benefit in terms of fun and enjoyment. Did fun and enjoyment fit with the company culture? Could we credibly claim the emerging category generics as our own?

So we looked within Paddy Power's walls to see how they ticked. And what a refreshing investigation it proved. Paddy Power does business with a smile. They're the bookies that offer odds on the Pope being Glasgow Rangers next signing. Nick Leeson opened their on-line service in Ireland. If our emotional benefit was all about the fun of betting, we saw that our communication would have inherent credibility. This was a brand promise which this company could live up to.

The need for fame

However, credible communication was a necessary but insufficient condition to gain consumer trust. And it was clear that for a new internet brand to become a direct transactions interface, it would need to be trusted – quickly. Adding 'Ireland's Biggest Bookies' in the logo would help. But more was needed.

And so we turned to the best shortcut to trust there is – fame. In a fragmented world, famous things unify people. They act as social glue. People trust famous stuff to help them navigate through life's increasingly complex journey. Why would people buy ISAs from a football club? Because Manchester United is famous. If Paddy Power could become famous and be a source of shared understanding and enjoyment, it would be trusted.

This meant that the content of the ads needed to be fame generating. No tailored message for a discrete audience. Our ads needed to provoke widespread debate within society at large. And no safe, middle-of-the-road subject matter. Infamy amongst some gets you fame amongst all. Getting our ads into conversation would give the brand a degree of scale and imbue it with trust.

The task-based brief

We now felt we had all the inputs we needed to share the task with the team. We had grasped the basic area that Paddy Power had to occupy, and satisfied ourselves that we could credibly own this high-ground position. We'd agreed upon a need for scale and fame. Instead of spending another week polishing our brief, we got into creative development.

We expressed the task as the central element: Make Paddy Power famous by associating it with the fun of betting on day-to-day extraordinary stuff. This would lead to the desired effect.

There were five elements which fed into the task:
- The product
- Key observations
- The brand
- The market
- The consumer

For each of these we provided relevant notes.

The creative development process

Planning's role in creative development was an iterative one. Instead of passing over the baton at a briefing and then disappearing until the creative review, we tried to jog alongside the creative team. We set up a string of collaborative sessions interspersed with occasional quiet time when we left the team alone.

We kept plying them with a stream of catalysts and comments. We showed them loads of clips of famous betting moments from film and TV. We made sure that they had plenty of bets on the Paddy Power site itself. We also took them down to the local bookies.

Beyond this we encouraged them to think wider. We were saying that Paddy Power was in the leisure business, and so we had to look at our competition as the broader leisure market. So we went down the pub and played on the fruit machines, we had an evening messing about on a Playstation and we dandered about a couple of multiplexes. We took them wrestling.

The first ideas defaulted to the 'oirish' approach. We all felt that this was missing the point somewhat. We really believed that the opportunity was there for Paddy Power to win the new high-ground of betting, not just some Irish slice of it. We also came to agree that the area of sport should be avoided. Our point about betting as a whole would be made far more effectively if we removed it from the expected world. And in any case, the world didn't need another football ad.

The campaign idea

As a group, we'd been thinking about those moments playing pool in the pub, or coming up the eighteenth when you decide to 'make things more interesting'. Betting in these moments is not about cash, it's about transforming the moment to get everyone involved.

This got us thinking about how pretty much every situation in life can be made more interesting if you look at it through the eyes of a betting man. Even the most mundane moments could be given a bit of added spice.

So this became the creative vehicle for the campaign. We took ordinary, day-to-day situations and livened them up by presenting them through a gambler's perspective. The campaign line – 'Let's make things more interesting' – stood as Paddy Power's rallying cry for a world livened up with more betting in it.

In choosing a carriage for our content, we again returned to our fame objective. We wanted big scale, public media, not narrow-cast channels. That meant posters and TV, not banner ads and take-away lids. The BACC wouldn't let us run normal TV ads, but we spotted that there'd been a recent relaxation of the sponsorship rules. We jumped at the chance to be on the biggest fame channel of them all.

The campaign therefore consisted of TV break bumpers, press ads, poster ads and viral animations.

The results

The business objectives for the communication were to raise awareness and drive traffic, and our strategy had been to achieve this through making the brand famous. And this is how things panned out.

Through its advertising the brand did indeed become famous. Indeed some would say infamous. The campaign had massive impact. Our bumpers went down a storm and the outdoor work received huge coverage in the press and TV. Five of the posters have been short-listed at the Campaign Poster awards. The sixth, *Grannies*, would have been an award winner too had a group of protesting OAPs in Bristol not held a vigil in front of it until it got banned. This episode in itself got our modest Irish dot.com on the front page of the tabloids and discussed in the broadsheets.

As a result of our campaign we drove traffic to the extent that Paddy Power's online customer base was increased by 116%. Moreover, the ads increased the online share of Power Leisure Group's turnover by 350%. Paddy Power proved to be that rare business phenomenon in 2001: a dot.com that made a profit.

The planning contribution

Planning's contribution to Paddy Power's success was pivotal. Both in terms of making the process quicker and getting better work out. Planning foresight identified future evolutions in the market and led to a re-definition of betting's benefit from rational cash to emotional fun. By interrogating the company, it then convinced everyone involved that we had credibility to go for the high ground and own future market generics. And through an understanding of the role that brands and cultural phenomena play in the lives of consumers, planning also persuaded them that fame was the best way of securing trust for Paddy Power.

Learning for the planning community

The Paddy Power tale gives pointers as to how planning might evolve in order to confront the challenges it faces – on a brand and industry level. By forgoing the planner's right to proposition writing time, and entering into a more fluid and collaborative relationship with the creative department, we were able to meet the brand challenge in this instance. We got better work out. Quicker. Through a shared understanding of the task. In so doing we helped renew the faith in planning and its continuing relevance in an ever faster, ever more demanding business world.

TV:

"Firemen won't let the siren spoil their enjoyment of Beat 106...."

Poster:

BRONZE
The Leith Agency

New brands or new advertisers
sponsor: Hall & Partners Europe

Now that's what I call a radio launch

This is a paper about how great advertising contributed to the successful launch of a new Scottish radio station, Beat 106. The planning solution moved on from the generic approach of identifying its music genre to one of celebrating it, and consequently from thinking about radio as a background medium. Beat 106 was too good to be wallpaper.

Winner: David Amers
Agency: The Leith Agency
Creative Director: Gerry Farrell
Art Director: Gareth Howells
Copywriter: Dougal Wilson
Client: Beat 106 FM
Product: Radio

"I love the 50s, don't you mate?"

"Absolutely mate. I think the 50s are totally drainpipemungus."

(DJs Smashie and Nicey)

Background

Beat 106 is a new regional radio station in central Scotland, launched in November 1999. Big Beat, the consortium behind the station, had won the coveted analogue licence with a commitment to an agenda of alternative (indie) rock and dance music. The commitment was not just to alternative music, it was also to more music; DJ's were to take a back seat. If people wanted inane commentary and Smashie and Nicey conversation they would have to tune in elsewhere to get it.

Launching a new radio station is tough and, at launch, the radio market in central Scotland was more crowded than ever. There were eleven Scottish local stations operating in Beat's area, as well as the nationals. Loyalty to these was very high in the west, 55% of the adult audience listened to Radio Clyde every week. In the east, 42% of adults tuned into Radio Forth.[1]

The brief

The advertising brief from the client was clear:
● Build awareness of Beat 106.
● Communicate that Beat 106 has a single-minded dedication to alternative rock and dance music.
● Generate trial (get people to tune in).

This brief incorporated one strong assumption – that to generate trial, we had to articulate the station's unique music policy.

Finding the right audience

The task to generate trial was complicated by the large and diverse nature of the commercial radio audience. This audience consists of teenagers and parents, men and women, 'opinion formers' and mass market 'followers'. All in all, people of every shade of musical preference.

It was not obvious, therefore, who the core target audience for the advertising should be (even for a station committed to alternative rock and dance music). After all, with the likes of The Clash, Travis and Coldplay regularly enjoyed by Radio Two listeners, it is obvious that the horizons of youth culture have broadened significantly.

We concluded from research made available to us by Beat 106 that the core audience should be 15-24 year olds, a segment who:
● Felt distanced from Radio One's perceived metropolitan, southern English bias.

- Viewed local commercial radio stations as narrow minded and parochial.
- Criticised both sets of stations for the 'poppy, teenybop' flavour of their output.

We aimed to excite a very specific audience – older teenagers and young adults into indie music and dance – to get them to tune into Beat 106. This was not an easy task given how self-consciously cool and dismissive of advertising this audience can be.

Initial briefing and creative work

Initially, there was general agreement that to achieve our objective, the advertising had to highlight the station's USP – its dedicated alternative music policy. The original proposition – "The Air Freshener" – allowed us to talk about all the fresh, new music which dominated the play list.

The initial creative briefing brought the station's music policy to life. It basically involved listening to indie stuff like The Manic Street Preachers, The Beta Band, Pulp, Stereophonics as well as plenty of dance music. The type of music that would never be played (boy bands, Britney, Billie, Steps etc) was also discussed but, thankfully, never played. The lively briefing felt like a good start.

However, problems with the brief soon became clear. The creatives found it very difficult to move beyond talking about the specific musical genres or, indeed, the likely featured artists. So, typically, we had press and poster headlines such as " So much jungle you'll need a machete" or "A Boyzone Free Zone". This was advertising clear on communication, low on excitement. For our discriminating and creatively literate target audience, this was never going to be enough.

Qualitative groups

To help us move forward, we conducted a number of groups amongst 18-24 year olds who fitted the Beat 106 profile: regular radio listeners into indie music and dance. We didn't want the usual suburban professional respondents so we recruited friends of staff who we knew fitted the profile perfectly.

As usual, we played around with techniques. One, in particular, proved very fruitful. Pairs were asked to illustrate and describe their perfect radio station. A clear consensus emerged around several key themes:

- Different types of music at different times of the day.
- Greater imagination and variety in the play list.
- More human DJs who avoid cheesy clichés and who are not egomaniacs.
- News and information that is relevant to young people living in Scotland.

The problem was that differences surfaced when we probed music content in detail. The alternative music scene is so fragmented nowadays that everyone's perfect radio station had very different music ingredients.

This insight highlighted a potential threat. By singling out specific music genres, we could alienate potential listeners before they had a chance to hear the station. This is exactly what our initial creative work was doing. The risk of misrepresentation was particularly acute since every new station needs to be given time to find its own voice.

Beat 106's dedication to indie and dance was the station's USP but, from an advertising point of view, it was a minefield strategically and a dead-end creatively. We had to change our approach.

Rethink

Our groups had shown that music playlist was the most divisive element of a radio station's offering and only part of what listeners were looking for. What they wanted was a station they could really engage with.

Knowing what they wanted was one thing, knowing what to tell them was another. The key insight came from thinking broadly about radio as a medium. Our research had shown that people wanted to actively listen to a radio station. We realised that this was not the way most people were used to experiencing radio. Even the Radio Advertising Bureau accepts that radio, unlike TV, is most often experienced as a passive, background medium.

It was by focussing upon this fact that the breakthrough was made. Radio stations are often background music, but Beat 106 was going to be too good for that.

From this thought process came a new proposition: "Beat 106: Foreground not background music."

We wanted to position Beat 106 in such a way that people would feel that they were missing something special if they didn't tune into 106. It didn't matter if they didn't know exactly what they were going to hear.

Planning insight led to a complete turn around in the creative brief.

The initial brief was: "Communicate music policy with a sense of excitement."

The new brief became: "Generate a sense of excitement and anticipation around the station itself – without talking about the music."

The creative work

The creatives found it a short walk from this new proposition to a strong creative idea: "People go to absurd lengths to reduce noise to listen to Beat 106". The idea was summed up neatly in the endline: "Ssh – It's Beat 106".

Two TV ads absurdly dramatised the consequences of listening to a station that foregrounds music – you simply don't want anything to interrupt it.

In the most popular of the TV ads, firemen race to an emergency using a hand-held "Mee Maw" sign in place of their loud siren. The firemen in the vehicle could all be seen nodding away to the music in true mates-in-a-GTI-with-a-sound-system fashion. It was a scenario our youthful target audience could immediately relate to and enjoy.

The TV was complemented by a series of striking six-sheet posters, T-sides and mega-rears on buses.

Media selection and timing

The advertising task demanded rapid coverage. Not surprisingly, TV was the lead medium. STV provided the coverage, supplemented with Channel 4 and Channel 5 macros to deliver the type of talked-about programming we required for credibility.

To add impact at street level, a six-sheet campaign was booked in proximity to universities, cinemas and clubs in Glasgow and Edinburgh. Bus mega-rears provided campaign longevity.

A conventional approach to media selection was ideal for our task. However, we took an unconventional approach to timing.

The client wanted, not unreasonably, for the advertising to coincide with the station's November launch. We decided against this for three reasons:
• Firstly, station programming and personalities take time to settle in and we wanted to let the station find its voice before we began advertising.
• Secondly, we were confident that the station would first be discovered by an audience of trendy young music enthusiasts, who would act as evangelists in selling their station to their peers. Advertising too early would inhibit this process.
• Thirdly, amongst the most important consideration for any new radio station is the publication of the industry standard (RAJAR) audience statistics. Audience share, as reported by RAJAR, can prove fundamental to a station's ability to attract advertisers and revenue, and hence, its survival.

Although the station went on air in November 1999, we timed our advertising to coincide with the December fieldwork for the RAJAR research.

With the vital RAJAR research period in mind, we developed the following three stage trial model. During November '99, Beat 106 would not be advertised, but communication would be left to 'trendies' and word of mouth. Then, advertising to the mainstream would go out from December through to February 2000. Then in March 2000 the audience would be 'oldies'.

In effect, we had a post brand launch advertising launch. (December 1999 to February 2000). This approach to timings didn't affect the creativity but it had a big impact on the campaign's success.

Results

Beat's target of achieving nine per cent weekly reach of all adults in the first year of operation was regarded as very ambitious by industry insiders. We in fact achieved 13% reach in the first quarter which, compared with reach achieved by station launches since 1994, made this the most successful regional radio launch ever in the UK. (46% of that reach was amongst the core target of 15-24s).

Over its first year, Beat's figures have consolidated, while its direct competitors have lost many thousands of listening hours, particularly amongst the 15-24s. Beat has grown its share of both the youth and all adults audience.

Independent research highlighted that our funny and relevant campaign had "made a major contribution to the successful launch of the station."

Within eight weeks the campaign had more than paid for itself through incremental advertising revenue and contributed substantially to the perceived value of the radio station. This was such that the original shareholders in Big Beat were able to sell the station for a profit of £32 million on an initial investment of only £2 million.

Summary

The planning decision to steer away from articulating Beat 106's dedicated music policy towards a more inspired view of the station – that unlike most radio, this was not going to be background music – liberated the brief and led to outstanding work loved by client, punters and peers.

"Finally, the best of the bunch. The 'fire engine' execution is a corker. Everyone I play it to laughs out loud. The timing is flawless. Want a prediction for 2000? We'll see kilts at the Grosvenor for this one."

(Larry Barker, *Campaign* Private View. 11th February, 2000).

[1] Source:RAJAR

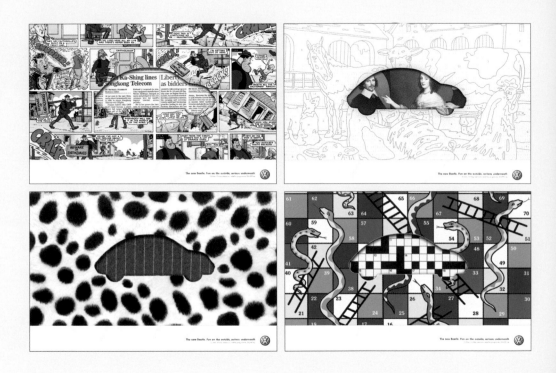

New brands or new advertisers
sponsor: Hall & Partners Europe

The New Beetle: taking fun seriously

Despite a successful launch without advertising, planning identified a role post-launch. Whilst people loved New Beetle, they also thought it overpriced, due to the misperception that it lacked engineering excellence. This misperception needed to be addressed, while maintaining the fun aspects derived from the car's appearance.

Winner: Matt Willifer
Agency: BMP DDB
Creative Directors: Dave Buchanan, Mike Hannett
Art Director: Justin Tindall
Copywriter: Adam Tucker
Client: Volkswagen UK
Product: New Beetle

Introduction

This paper will show how we found a role for advertising, even when all the initial signs suggested there wasn't one, and went on to produce a brief that not only reconciled two seemingly irreconcilable communications tasks, but also provided a powerful creative inspiration on account of this. In so doing, we wrote a strategy that seemingly flew in the face of the dictum that 'advertising can only communicate one thing.'

There isn't a problem

The New Beetle was launched in the UK to great acclaim in January 2000. It was a concept car made into reality, based on the most popular car ever, and powered by a Golf two-litre GTi engine. It received acres of PR space. Just before its launch 90% of people knew it existed, even though it didn't. It sold like extremely hot cakes, and everyone seemed to love it.

And all for a total advertising spend of zero.

If ever there was a car that did not need advertising support and would not win BMP an APG award, here it was.

It would have been easy to get carried away. However we had a few nagging doubts drawn from various sources:

1. Artificially inflated demand: initially demand was, in a sense, artificially inflated, not just because of the transitory honeymoon period that inevitably surrounds hyped cars, but also because initial sales were satisfying a year of pent up demand via the order bank.

2. The German experience: we talked to DDB International about the New Beetle in Germany (launched a year and a half prior to the UK.) There, after a big sales peak after launch, they were struggling to reach target.

3. Does popularity equal sales? Whilst everyone seemed to love the New Beetle, anecdotally people were less sure whether they would actually buy one. As one of my friends remarked: "It's great, but it's not really my thing."

Whilst there might not have been a problem, and whilst there was no obvious role for advertising, we felt we should not take the continuing health of New Beetle for granted. So, we had Millward Brown cut relevant data against potential New Beetle drivers, and Volkswagen allowed us to conduct some qualitative research. Given the findings we were very glad we did.

Identifying a problem before it was a problem

The research for the most part played back to us what we already knew. Yes the New Beetle was top of mind for people. Yes they adored it. Yes they loved the fun, eye-catching shape.

However, there were also indications there could be a serious problem after the initial honeymoon period. One quote summed it up: "I've heard it's about sixteen grand. I think it's a lovely car, but that's very expensive for what it is."[1]

Why? It was not that these people couldn't afford New Beetle. The sample we recruited for the qualitative could afford one by definition. Lots of cars cost £16k or more, and this was the most loved car in the country. And more than that it was also excellently engineered: based on the Golf platform, and powered by a top of the range Golf two-litre GTi engine. The equivalent Golf was actually more expensive.

However, crucially, people didn't know it was an excellent car powered by a top of the range engine! After all, the PR centred on the car's appearance. And, because of its appearance, people were inclined to believe it was (for want of a better phrase) all mouth and no trousers. The New Beetle was having the same problem as an intelligent blonde.

Being a 'proper' car mattered greatly to the kind of people willing to spend £16k on a car. They might like it as the 'in thing', but research suggested that in many ways this just compounded the problem. No one likes to feel they are being duped into paying for this year's fad. They might want to drive a smile, but certainly not a joke. Another respondent said: "I like it but I wouldn't buy one. If I buy a car I have to know I'm getting a good car – not that."

The quantitative research supported this. Spontaneous impressions showed that 15% thought the car to be overpriced whilst none thought it to be reasonably priced. Further, the most salient features were to do with looks and character and unusually for a Volkswagen, well-engineered and reliability were almost nowhere in sight.

So, despite all evidence to the contrary, we had identified a role for advertising. The mass of PR and the car's appearance were only telling half the story. If the rush for New Beetles subsided, advertising was to tell people about New Beetle's engine, justify the price premium, and hence give them the ammunition they needed to buy a car they loved.

Hang on, we're advertising the New Beetle here

However, there was something about this direction that seemed at odds with the wonderful, carefree New Beetle brand. People did after all genuinely love it. And they loved it because of what it looked like. It made them smile. It brightened up their day. And yet we wanted to talk about its engineering? Had we analysed ourselves into a corner and lost sight of common sense?

Whilst we did want to talk about engineering, for three key reasons we also wanted to retain the side of New Beetle that people loved.

1. Branding: by itself, there was nothing about engineering that linked to the New Beetle brand. At worst, by being serious, we could even taint the carefree brand

149

that people loved so much.

2. Distinctiveness: every car manufacturer and its dog had campaigns about engines and performance. It was not this that would make either the New Beetle or its advertising unique.

3. Appeal: advertising about cars' engines could be so dull. The onus was upon us to provide a brief that would intuitively lead to appealing and impactful advertising.

In a nutshell, we were worried that in talking about New Beetle's engineering we would have a strategy that stacked up well in a PowerPoint presentation, but not in the real world. It just couldn't be right to produce a generic sounding brief for one of the least generic cars.

Making two things into one

So we wanted to do two things. First, we wanted to talk about New Beetle's engineering. Second, we wanted to talk about its fun, unusual appearance. But we also wanted to give our creatives a single-minded brief. So, did we have to choose between them?

Well, a first obvious solution was to ask creatives to write about engines but do so in a fun tone. However, this would have been a cop out. The fact it was fun had nothing to do with the engineering. It was to do with what it looked like – and it was referencing this that was key to representing the brand. And anyway, we did not want to pass the buck: "Here is something very dull and generic. Please spice it up a bit."

However, there was a way to combine both the fun look of the car and the engineering story into a single, well-branded and distinctive strategy. There was one consumer quote that got us thinking: "OK, if you're telling me it's a good car I'll believe you, but I'm pretty surprised – it looks like it's exactly the opposite."

This was the key. The car's engineering and its appearance were not just any two things. Looked at the way this respondent had, they were exact opposites: the engineering was serious, the appearance fun. There was a contradiction at the heart of the brand that we could exploit. Our brief could both be about both the engine and the appearance.

But what about the old dictum that a piece of advertising can only effectively communicate one thing?

Well, we realised that sometimes there is an opportunity to communicate two things in a brief, if and only if those two things have a clearly defined relationship to each other – in this case exact opposites thrust together.

Or looked at another way, the advert would communicate two things, but be about one thing: the surprising and striking juxtaposition of two opposites.

Realising this was the key to our success. Rules are made to be broken if there is good enough reason. But ultimately the proof of this lies less in these words than in the brilliance and clarity of the creative work.

A catalyst for creative excellence

The campaign Adam Tucker and Justin Tindall created was brilliant – the kind you take one look at and know instantly you've got something special.

In each ad we see the outline of a New Beetle. Each ad centres on a theme (e.g. games), with a fun example outside (e.g. Snakes and Ladders), and a serious example inside (e.g. a crossword). The line reads: "The New Beetle. Fun on the outside, serious underneath", with the support line: "2 litre 115 bhp"

It was both immensely clear and strategically sound (indeed the end-line was almost identical to the proposition), but at the same time they added clearly that magic ingredient to create a very lateral and visual idea. The brief seemed to act as a catalyst for an astoundingly creative piece of work.

With the ads written, Volkswagen's media agency Mediacom came up with the idea of special builds, using real fur (outside) and pinstripe (inside). Just as creatives used the brief to jump to the juxtaposition between fun and serious images, so Mediacom used this basic idea to jump to the juxtaposition between fun and serious materials. Their solution was excellent, and led to the additional boost of PR.

Success

In summer 2000, although sales were still reasonable, the order bank and the PR slowed. It was time to shoot and run the advertising. Press ran in mid-July until the beginning of September, with poster activity for the last two weeks of this.

The effect was marked. The campaign won one of the highest accolades in the world: the Clio Grand Prix. It was also nominated for D&AD, and won at th Campaign press and poster awards.

Amongst our key target audience (defined on our tracking study as those who express an interest in New Beetle and are planning to spend at least £15k on their next car) awareness of the campaign was incredible – way beyond expectations for a print campaign. Prompted ad awareness for press – high anyway given PR – shot from 38% to 52%[2] . For posters, awareness shot from a 12% base to an incredible 23%[3].   And it was saying the right things – spontaneous perceptions of being overpriced almost halved, whilst perceptions of reliability/build increased significantly[4] .

Anecdotal feedback from consumer groups (and Volkswagen's retailer network) was excellent. "It's really bright compared with most posters – really catches your eye." "It's saying that it's a wacky kind of car, but remember it's made by Volkswagen so it's good as well."

Conclusions

Planning's contribution can be summarised in three steps.

First, we were proactive in using research to identify a role for advertising, even though all evidence suggested there wasn't one. The role was to advertise New Beetle's engineering credentials.

Second, we realised that whilst this appeared strategically sound, it seemed somehow wrong for this fun and visually arresting car.

Third, we reconciled these different directions into one, by noting that its carefree appearance and excellent engineering could be seen as exact opposites. The brief centred on this unexpected juxtaposition. Hence we showed advertising could say two things provided they had a clearly defined relationship to each other. If I had to pick one main learning from this paper, this would be it. The creative was on brief but had definitely added that creative magic, that leap. As such, it not only vied for the world's most prestigious creative awards, but also raised consumer awareness of the relevant issues.

[1] BMP exploratory qualitative work - as are all following quotes.
[2] Four week rolling data: 17 July (pre-figure), 4th September (during/post figure).
[3] Four week rolling data: 14 August (pre-figure), 4th September (during/post figure).
[4] Source: Millward Brown.

Multi-market Campaigns

The APG Creative Planning Awards

The APG Awards demonstrate that great planning can lead to great creative work. At The Nursery we see research the same way: we believe, along with Planning's founders Stephen King and Stanley Pollitt, that involving the consumer, the end user, in the creative development process early on can make the result more powerful. Research shouldn't be an obstacle to great creative work, it should be a help. Good research is a necessary part of great planning.

The Nursery
1 Wardour Mews, London W1F 8AH
Telephone: 020 7734 1166   www.the-nursery.net

Brand Endline

Poster: "There's no such thing as failure, there's only giving up."

TV: Roberto Baggio's Walk

GOLD

Bartle Bogle Hegarty

Multi-market campaigns
sponsor: The Nursery

'Keep Walking': The journey back to icon status

This paper shows how regional and separate briefs for different variants went on to produce a single communications campaign for Johnnie Walker running in 210 countries. Classic pitch planning made the single campaign possible by clarifying the brief, its aims, the category and brand truths, the creative possibilities and the opportunities to make the most of the creative idea.

Winners: Ben King, Dorothea Gartland
Agency: Bartle Bogle Hegarty
Creative Director: John O'Keeffe
Art Directors: Various
Copywriters: Various
Client: Guinness UDV
Product: Johnnie Walker

What is the story about?

This is the story of a journey. The journey from separate briefs for Red and Black Labels to a masterbrand campaign for Johnnie Walker. The journey from a solution for only seven markets, to work running in 210 countries around the world. The journey from a print and TV campaign in November 1999 to a total communications campaign covering everything from PR to sponsoring the first unsupported team walk to the North Pole. The journey from inspiring progress to actually enabling it by developing funds in different countries which help people to realise their dreams. The journey from interrupting content to generating it ourselves in the shape of 42 sponsored programmes now running on *CNN* and *Discovery*.

It is a journey that has led to a campaign that has united the Johnnie Walker marketing community around the world with a common purpose.

It is a journey that has seen Johnnie Walker go on to lead the category not simply in volume but also in terms of values.

Finally it is a journey of brand success.

This is the story of 'Keep Walking'

This isn't the story of how one major insight led inexorably to a single creative solution. Rather, it looks at how disparate planning skills were simultaneously needed to deliver the solution.

We've called this a story of total planning - like in the '70s when the Dutch ruled the world with their total approach to football – where a team of people were flexible and worked together.

Pitch planning

It is in fact a story of pitch planning – putting lots of balls in the air, asking and answering the right questions, linking one thought to another until everything falls into place.

We're going to talk about seven different steps in planning – carried out by different members of the agency/client team, all of which led us to the territory of progress expressed through *Keep Walking*.

What exactly is the task?

Johnnie Walker came to us with ambitious goals and tough challenges, yet both Red and Black Label were in decline. In an age long before the advent of the telephone let alone jet travel and global communications, Johnnie Walker was the world's first, globally available brand. According to the Johnnie Walker brand guide: "Johnnie Walker was in 120 countries before Coke left America".

But whilst Johnnie Walker was still the most profitable spirits brand in the world, it had lost its mantle as the world's premier brand. With the rise of white spirits it had also ceased by 1999 to be rated by Interbrand as the most powerful spirit (it had been overtaken by both Bacardi and Smirnoff in that year).

The challenge to us was not just to sell more whisky, but to develop a big idea which would make Johnnie Walker a global icon again.

Alberto Gavazzi, marketing director of Johnnie Walker, Brazil established the challenge: "I want Johnnie Walker to step out and lead the male target."

Our first task, then, was to force debate about what these ambitions really meant. What is a global icon? What is leadership?

What is a global icon? We debated this question until both we and the client agreed on the following points: Johnnie Walker would need to turn itself into a brand which had values people could identify with; it needed a role in their lives.

What is leadership? To help define 'leadership' we analysed Johnnie Walker's early success. In the early years, Johnnie Walker had evangelised Scotch whisky around the world. It did not confine itself to considering where it sat versus other whiskies. More recently whisky had suffered from a lack of such leadership versus white spirits and had hence declined. We argued that leadership must be borne out of not just dominating your category, but also in being able to lead your category's challenge against others. Not by aping the others, but by finding out what was special about whisky and the brand.

Establishing these parameters gave us the room to develop very different, globally iconic work.

What is the big idea?

The client asked us for a big idea, but although this is a commonly-used phrase, there was no clear definition of what it meant.

So some of the team set out to analyse the work of ten global icon brands and put together a presentation setting out a series of objectives for our big idea based on what others had achieved.

- Be rooted in a simple, powerful brand truth.
- Break the mould.
- Redefine the category the brand is in.
- Capture the imagination.
- Be campaignable and extendable beyond advertising.
- Become valued company-wide.
- Become famous.
- Turn awareness into insistence.

This work was developed with and presented back to the creative teams, ensuring we were talking in a common language, and making sure everyone understood how big our expectations were.

How does the category talk about Itself?

This started as an exercise intended to identify the clichés of the category's advertising and involved one member of the team sitting in a room for two days whilst looking at over 2,300 global and local ads for competitive whiskies. But not only did it stake out what areas the creatives should avoid, it also led to a much better understanding of what the category believed it stood for, culminating in one simple board.

The board showed 'the rules of advertising' with the 'product role' as punctuation (the end or the beginning), or as part of the occasion or as a catalyst. 'Imagery' included men together, a man (hero), a woman (object), a glass with ice, Scottish scenery and a pack. 'Themes and positionings' included savoir faire, wealth, business success, discernment, friendship and heritage.

Despite looking at all these campaigns for different brands and types of whiskies, it was almost as if the end-frames were interchangeable. Almost all insisted on combining some sort of product message with an idealised and aspirational user and occasion.

Not only did the majority of brands talk about the same thing, they also did it in the same way. There was a requirement to include both a pack shot and a drinking scene, and almost every execution had the look and feel of a commercial from the late 70s or early 80s. So similar, in fact, that in many ways the category of Scotch had become the brand.

In terms of how whisky defined its purpose in people's lives, there was also a very clear product role. It was almost invariably the catalyst or reward for success, a clichéd badge of having made it.

Since the category behaved in such a consistent, and dated, way it was easy to know what clichés to avoid. The creative challenge was to try and avoid them without reinventing what whisky was all about.

What is the emotional high ground?

At the same time, other members of the team were ploughing through the usual mountain of previous research.

This confirmed whisky's masculine values and link to achievement. Usage imagery showed consumers either drank or gifted it as a reward or celebration of their success.

Whisky was becoming associated with people who had reached the end of their journey and were now sitting back to enjoy a whisky and reminisce about it.

This made one document we came across particularly interesting. It had been commissioned by UDV as a step back from the detail of whisky. Its aim was to understand the changing cultural values surrounding masculinity and to look at what trends united men (our target) around the world. It enabled us to understand what success had come to mean at the end of the twentieth century. All around the world men were recognising that success was not just about material achievements or improving their status. It wasn't only about the destination – the journey was just as important.

"No-one really grows from having a Mercedes or a beach house – it's about family, friends... no-one's ever done everything, never learnt it all," (male Venezuelan respondent, 50 years old).

Success was now being defined in more disparate ways. So much so that the word itself was no longer appropriate. A much better term was progress.

In progress we felt we had a fresh, contemporary take on the emotional area that global consumers linked to whisky: a take which would liberate our creatives.

What is creatively fertile?

In order to understand what territories would be able to generate great work, the creative department had been involved from the moment we took the brief – travelling with us around the world and being involved in strategic discussions.

As per the pitch brief we began by asking for different routes for Red and Black, and by using two boards. The first showed the two key attributes: for Red it was male bonding; for Black it was a symbol of success.

The second board was borne of members of the pitch team spending time carrying out classic brand archaeology, including trips to the brand home, the archive, distilleries involved in its production and the bottling plant. It showed 'Johnnie Walker's brand truths' with information about its heritage authenticity, quality, global renown and iconic values.

The challenge was to explain how the variant emotional values might be linked with brand properties.

A number of routes were subsequently developed, concentrating on different areas. These were used to help us to refine and clarify our thinking. They were: using the colours as properties by variant; exploring heritage; linking back to product features; and icon attributes – the name, the slanting logo, the square bottle and the striding man.

These routes were all shared with the client and as a team we agreed that, whilst many were funny or good, none was a big idea when measured against the criteria we had set ourselves.

Some focussed too heavily on the brand attributes and so lacked emotional power, others were not big enough to lead the category or make Johnnie Walker into an icon.

However a creative truth emerged: the best work focussed on the most iconic attributes - common to both Red and Black - the square bottle, the slanting label, the name and most of all the 'striding man', one of the most recognised branding

163

devices in the world. This led us to renew our focus on another area, an area that had troubled the team from the start.

What is the brand?

At the time Johnnie Walker was marketed as a series of variants, each competing against different sectors of the whisky market. The main variants were Red and Black Label and over time they had become the brands. Each had a different marketing team, and at the time of the pitch, each had a different communications brief.

During the pitch an argument developed that concentration on the variants had a reductive affect on what was deemed to be the competition, so Black competed against Chivas Regal and Red competed against Dewars. It had a reductive affect on the marketing spend and effort. It had a reductive affect on Johnnie Walker's ability to lead whisky's competition against other sectors.

Early on some of the team began to question whether to be iconic, we should concentrate on Johnnie Walker rather than just Red or Black. Concentrating on a single brand would allow us to focus on the core emotional territory of progress. Also our work so far with creatives had shown that it was the icons common to both that were the most compelling, and that one in particular stood out: the striding man. We were aware of him as a dandy figure and as a representation of Johnnie Walker, but with the creative interest in him, we began to ask why he was called the 'striding' man, and why he had been central to Johnnie Walker advertising up until the 1960s. We discovered that he had been designed in 1908 to represent the pioneering and entrepreneurial zeal of the Walker family – hence 'striding'.

The creative leap: in retrospect this sounds very simple, but the big step was that the creative team were quick to bring together the progress of Johnnie Walker as the pioneer – expressed through the 'striding man' – with the emotional territory of progress.

This connection first led to a creative thought called 'Walk the walk'. But going back to our earlier debate we believed that to be globally iconic Johnnie Walker needed to be more pro-active, to be a verb, to inspire rather than just reflect people's progress.

And so late one night a couple of weeks before the pitch date the idea was pushed to become an imperative – to become '*Keep Walking*'.

How do you make the client a co-creator?

The team travelled around the world sharing strategic and creative developments at every stage. The 'Sizing the Task' discussion was had in Brazil, Colombia, Greece and Venezuela as well as London. The 'big idea' presentation also travelled, with local clients asked to add to the definition. Creative work was also presented in meetings around the world. As a result, local teams were encouraged to think about Johnnie Walker in a new context and to understand the direction we were moving in.

Without this level of involvement, from a diverse range of markets, it would have been impossible for us to develop the type of work we wanted for the brand. This co-creation finally came to fruition in February 2000 at a workshop attended by the global Johnnie Walker community in Bangkok. Here they were invited to brainstorm ideas for *Keep Walking* and came up with three key initiatives beyond advertising – a fund, global content creation and global media. The experience encouraged them to think of themselves as guardians of the campaign. It is this that has led to so many of the developments and local expressions of *Keep Walking*.

Conclusion

This has been a story about pitch planning. Not a series of sequential steps, but a story about asking the right questions and gradually getting the right answers. This is a story about the value planning offers in clearing the way for creatives and in agreeing the end goal.

It is a story that shows the importance of real debates – to ensure agency and client are aiming for the same thing.

But mostly it's a story about getting different processes and pieces of thinking to fit together and help each other.

It would be very easy to claim that it had been one clear sequential process in which one revelation led to another. A process in which we identified the category's emotional heartland and found a brand truth with which to own it. But we hope you agree the true story is more interesting, and hope you enjoyed the journey.

TV: "During your period, your body temperature is ever so slightly higher ... this actually affects your sleep."

Press:

SILVER
D'Arcy

Multi-market campaigns
sponsor: The Nursery

Knowledge is always power

A new kind of fem-care advertising was created as a direct result of planning's recognition that P&G knows more about the female body than anyone else. In a market where product innovation has become less distinctive, this fact about the company behind the brand could be used to propel Always into a clear lead once again in consumers' eyes.

Winner: Ali Bucknall
Agency: D'Arcy
Creative Director: Nick Hastings
Art Director: Mim Sorrentino
Copywriter: Maddy Morris
Client: Procter & Gamble
Product: Always

167

Always – talking your body language

When I found out that I was to work on fem-pro my heart sank. Tight white pants and blue goo. How horrible. How depressing. How totally uninspiring. How not to get on in advertising.

How childish.

When I stopped whingeing and began to learn a bit more about the category I discovered something shocking. Periods are fascinating. No really they are. OK, maybe not the mucky stuff, but the bits behind it, the biology, the cycle – the why we are what we are sort of thing. And here's where it gets really interesting. Procter & Gamble, the makers of Always, know more about periods and the menstrual cycle than any doctor or medical establishment anywhere.

Our story starts when this was still a hidden truth. Planning dug deep to find this truth and used it as the basis for a fresh advertising idea that resonated with all women irrespective of their age or nationality.

In the beginning were bricks

Before Always came to Europe in the early 1990s women had to put up with large wadges of compressed cotton wool in their pants every month. Not very comfortable and very constraining. The arrival of Always Ultra turned the market on its head: pads that protected better than a 'brick' yet which were incredibly slim and discreet and advertising that talked openly about periods on television for the first time (somewhat radically for then).

Not surprisingly, the combination of radical products and a new approach to advertising helped to propel Always to market dominance in virtually every market in which it was launched. Ongoing innovation has helped it become the world's leading brand of feminine protection. This is a functional category where performance really does matter. There are no second chances. There is too much emotional anxiety about performance for any brand to move away from demonstrating its efficacy for too long without suffering share loss.

Although Always' early success had come about by simply demonstrating how well it works, over time, the combination of competitive products that looked similar and advertised in the same old way meant that there was little to distinguish one brand from another in women's eyes.

So our challenge was this. How can we continue to communicate the functional performance on which the brand has been built yet find a way of doing it more distinctively? And in doing so, ensure that it could travel across borders?

It started with a question

What were we already doing well and what could we learn from this? Our advertising to teens was felt to be particularly effective. So our senior client asked what it was about our advertising to teens that seemed to work so well. Perhaps this could be a useful starting place?

The Always *Knickers* campaign had run for several years in teen press. It simply demonstrated in a warm, witty and appropriate way the benefit of Always' better protection and was often cited as a favourite amongst teens. In addition, P&G's educational programme covering puberty, periods and growing up, was felt to help teens understand themselves better to enable them to manage their periods more effectively.

What if we could replicate this sense of helpfulness and engaging advertising in a way that would encompass all women?

Time to do some digging

We asked our clients whether there was any information about periods that might be appropriate for a wider audience. Amongst some of the things we were sent was a speech from a senior member of the fem-pro team in the US. Aside from being genuinely interesting, the question that sprang to mind was, "how come he knows so much?" So we asked for some more information and were sent even more interesting facts and figures. And the more we asked – the more we received. We appeared to have hit on something.

The goldmine

However it wasn't the information itself that interested us but what it revealed about P&G. We had unearthed a real nugget about the company that made Always. We discovered that P&G knows more about periods and the menstrual cycle than anyone else in the world. They fund more research, conduct more tests, talk to more women and help to educate more young girls than anyone. Quite simply, no one knows more about the female hormonal cycle than P&G.

The reason for this is that P&G believes that you can't make the best products without understanding and investigating exactly what part they play in a consumer's life. And this means understanding the totality of the menstrual cycle – how you feel mentally as well as physically. Consequently they had acquired a vast amount of knowledge over the years: knowledge that had inspired product innovation. We began to wonder whether the same knowledge, untapped by advertising could inspire brand communications.

Moreover, because understanding the essence of a woman – i.e. her menstrual cycle – is something that is of interest to all women, here was something that could resonate with women all over the world. But first we needed to make sure that the facts and figures we were hearing about were genuine and could sustain advertising. Time to visit the goldmine.

Visiting the goldmine

We spoke to company experts in the UK, Germany, Italy and the US. We read articles, books and interviewed women about their periods. The more we learned, the more excited we got. This was an unbelievably big area – we had no idea that P&G knew so much. Some of it was practical and useful while other facts were just extraordinary. All of the information combined to make us feel more knowledgeable about ourselves. If we felt that, then we were sure that women would feel the same when they were exposed to it. For example we discovered that:

- You start to menstruate when you have reached a certain body weight and fat content.
- The average age of menarche (onset of menstruation) has fallen as we get fatter – from 17, 100 years ago to 12 today.
- Menopause is puberty in reverse.
- You are more likely to get bigger tips when you are ovulating (if you are a waitress).
- Cravings for chocolate are really your body's way of telling you that you're low on magnesium.
- You can gain up to 7lbs of extra fluid during your period as your body retains water.
- You are born with a lifetime's supply of eggs.
- The time from ovulation to the onset of menstruation is consistent at 14 days – irrespective of the overall cycle length.
- You are more likely to be attracted to macho men when you ovulate and more homely types when you menstruate.
- Eating turkey can help ease PMT.
- Purchase intent may change according to where a woman is in her cycle.

And so on and so on. The list was endless – the more we learned the more there was to know. And the more interested we became. The trick now was to channel this knowledge into creative work that would have the same impact on our consumers as it did on us – i.e. to make us feel that if P&G knew all this stuff, they must really know what's what when it comes to products. Whilst not all of this information was cast iron fact or rather, categorically proven fact, it was sufficient to make us believe that there was something we could tap into and take to our consumers.

Our objective was to strengthen the feeling that Always makes the best performing products. Our creative strategy was to share with women the expert knowledge that P&G has about women and their bodies.

The proposition was simple: 'Because Always is the expert on a woman's cycle and all aspects of periods, you can trust it to make the best products.'

We wanted a creative solution that could take this sentiment across any medium in any country to any woman.

The creative solution

The creative solution was simple and yet it challenged the category conventions with a fresh new approach. It demonstrated that Always understands you inside and out summarised with the line "Always talks your body's language". Even though this works particularly well in English, the sentiment was recognised in all languages.

We produced a wide range of creative work ranging from interesting facts about the menstrual cycle in general to more specific period claims. Very radically for Always, some of the executions failed to show products. Yet each and every ad demonstrated that Always understands women. Very simply, the advertising highlights a fact relating to periods and/or the cycle, explains it and offers a solution either in terms of product and/or in the form of advice on what you can do to help yourself.

The advertising covered a wide range of different areas ranging from chocolate cravings to cramps, to intuition, to water retention and so on. More to the point, for a company whose lifeblood is innovation, we managed to show that product upgrades were born out of Always' understanding of women. For instance, the fact that your temperature rises during a period can impact on your sleep making you more restless (moving around 50 times a night), which is why Always' new Night pad has longer, flexible wings to keep you protected no matter how much you move about.

It's an idea that crosses all media and countries

With an idea that is bigger than advertising alone but is more about the brand, the answer was to think more creatively about the media used to reflect that. If you want people to think differently about you, you need to behave differently. And so we did.

The campaign included TV, women's press for more 'intimate' conversations, washroom posters to engage women at a time when they were a literal captive audience, postcards, and a new medium never used before: the wrappers of the products themselves.

All of which makes this a campaign which not only challenged category conventions but which has turned fem-pro advertising around. It has changed from something many women were still embarrassed about to something that is often mentioned spontaneously in groups as something they enjoy watching or reading.

A sure-fire consumer hit

The advertising is running in the UK, Germany and France and has been researched in a number of different countries to test its overall acceptability. The potential is enormous.

● We have tapped into an extremely powerful universal truth that has the flexibility to adapt to local cultural and market needs . Irrespective of country, age or lifestage, women are fascinated by themselves and their bodies. And here is a brand that truly understands this and gives them the means to know themselves better. And what's more, if Always really understands women, it probably makes really good products.

● But don't just take my word for it. These are some of the comments made during research[1].

● "You would presume that they researched the subject in depth to give you adverts like that, so therefore you trust that their product is better because they've researched into other times of your cycle, so you'd presume that they've researched into what's best to use."

● "They're not just making the product and selling it to you. They're also taking the time out to find relevant facts and information … [it makes me]…trust them, trust their products".

● "I'd expect Always to do it…because they've always been first…and they're big.. I think the others will copy won't they?"

● "It's not like a normal advert is it when they're all prancing about in white trousers."

● "I'd enjoy watching it."

● "It's really different."

Overall, a big 'thumbs-up' from the women of Europe. And a feeling of satisfaction for us.

[1] Source: qualitative research amongst 16-34 year-old women in UK, France and Germany, May 2000 /December 2001

"It's the boss, so what are you going to do ... let him score? ... Beware of the voices."

"So your salary negotiations are going badly, can he smell your fear?... Beware of the voices."

BRONZE
Saatchi & Saatchi

Multi-market campaigns
sponsor: The Nursery

Unleashing a monster brand

Monster.com, a US internet job site, wanted to bring its vision to Europe. Planning's core discovery was that although work cultures differed across Europe, everyone felt work was accelerating and becoming less comfortable. No-one wanted to admit discomfort and show weakness. They had nowhere to turn. Enter Monster.com. It became a career adviser, not just a jobs page.

Winner: Craig Mawdsley
Agency: Saatchi & Saatchi
Creative Director: Dave Droga
Art Director: Nik Studzinski
Copywriter: Gavin Kellett
Client: Monster.com
Product: Monster.com

175

A brave new world

At the end of the twentieth century, the world changed.

Now we would work on 'internet time'. Any bright teenager could become a millionaire overnight. Cash flow and profits were old-fashioned. This was the biggest thing since the industrial revolution. If you doubted this, you just didn't get it, man, you were a dinosaur.

Oh what a brave new world of advertising this was. The US led the way, website names were tattooed on toddlers, and attack dogs were loosed on marching bands. Over here a range of award-winning and esoteric work was unleashed. People fell in love with the benefits of the internet as a delivery mechanism – everything you've ever wanted, but faster and easier! Brand values seemed a little old-fashioned.

It's difficult to recall just how tough it was to go against the prevailing wisdom.

Surely advertising was entering a golden age. Creativity was given free rein whilst still generating riches for clients. Yet, back in the summer of the year 2000 we took a long hard look at the issues facing Monster.com and decided that 'look at me' advertising wouldn't be a long-term solution. We looked beyond the benefits of the delivery mechanism to find insights. We constructed a brand rooted in fundamental values that generated effective creativity.

If that sounds easy, then you probably never worked on a dot com brief.

A little bit of history

Monster.com was established in the US in 1994, getting its esoteric name from the concept of advertising jobs on the internet on a 'monster' scale. It had made a big splash with famous advertising and became well known from Ohio to Oregon. The founder of the company could talk about becoming as famous and meaningful as Nike without sounding like a crackpot.

At this time in the US everyone and their grandma was on the internet, 10 year-olds dealt in Wall Street stocks and everyone had a website. Creating an internet brand was just a case of achieving name recognition. People embraced new brands, as they were part of the revolution themselves – most of the customers were shareholders, keen to see their stock rising.

Monster.com shared the world-changing ambition of many of its dot com counterparts – it had a vision "to take people further by revolutionising the world of work". Moreover, it wanted to bring this vision to Europe.

The challenge of Europe

Monster.com arrived in Europe as the internet was extending beyond geeks. It established sites in a few countries, but in the year 2000, their ambitions grew. It wanted a single campaign for Europe, taking existing markets further and launching everywhere else. We were appointed as its European agency and immediately faced some challenges:

1. The internet – big in America, new in Europe. You wouldn't find too many grandmas in Seville dealing stocks on the internet. For that matter, you wouldn't find too many teenagers in Berlin buying CDs on it either. The internet was full of promise, but most were still suspicious about using it for personal or financial matters. Europe was going through the 'wait and see' phase.

2. Europe – single market, multiple cultures. Creating a brand in the US is not easy, but at least there is (largely) a common language and shared values. Europe is not like that; people have different cultures and a strong attachment to their country's unique place in the world. We've all seen (and sometimes created) 'lowest common denominator' advertising that tries to avoid offending any of them.

3. The world of work – worlds apart. In Germany you arrive at nine and leave at five thirty. Once your company has hired you they won't fire you. Employment legislation and strong unions largely prevent redundancies. Hence companies take a lot of time and trouble to select staff and make few hirings. In the UK, there is little employment legislation to stop the employer firing you at the drop of a hat. So, you start at eight and stay until seven with a rushed sandwich at lunch, and still manage to be the least productive workers in Europe. This list could continue, but the point is made. International advertising is tough. International advertising about work and jobs is tougher.

At this point we had an interesting notion. Everyone else was doing 'dot com' advertising. What if we looked beyond the benefits of the internet and tried to define unique values for the brand? What if we forgot this was a dot com?

This is not a dot com

All our competitors were dot coms, and made a show of it.

There was one main international competitor, Stepstone, and a host of local competition. There were local internet start-ups, sites funded by newspapers (the home of traditional job advertising and keen to ensure they didn't miss out on the internet) and extensions of existing portals, like Yahoo, or MSN. They boasted of search facilities and e-mail updates. However, this seemed to make them all seem fairly similar, as they could all do the same stuff for job seekers.

If we were able to show insight and understanding into the consumer, (just like a normal brand would), people may be inclined to trust us more. In fact, more advertising driven by generic dot com benefits was the last thing we needed, as people in Europe were still sceptical about the internet. We were, after all, expecting them to do some risky things here, like send us their CV or register their interest in leaving their current job. If this stuff got out then they would be pretty embarrassed. They were only likely to share such information with a brand they trusted.

The search for brand values would have to be rooted in authenticity, so we started at the beginning and interrogated the product and service. The dot com hype would have you believe that people had been replaced by servers and search engines, but we had a hunch that the people and their ideas would make the difference.

A visit to the Monster.com office was revealing. It was a rare time when the corporate mission statement ("to take people further by revolutionising the world of work") was born out of the desire and passion of the employees, not grafted on by corporate managers. It was a curious combination of dot com enthusiasm and bricks and mortar professionalism. If we could bottle this and sell it around Europe as a brand we would be on to a winner.

Listening to the consumer

And here we needed more help. We weren't going to unite those diverse national cultures by conjecturing from our offices in London. We needed research to find out if there were any commonalties.

The interviews we conducted around Europe all began with the expected cultural differences. It got interesting when we saw beyond the differences.
Our first insight was that everyone was feeling the pace of change.
Everyone was feeling less secure. People worried about keeping their skills fresh to compete with younger generations. They were also all experiencing the emergence of new technologies – some were excited, but many had a fear about what the future would hold. It was also clear that despite varying levels of formality in workplaces across Europe, old conventions were disappearing and previous certainties falling away.

They knew they could do better than their current job, but worried about the uncertainty of moving.

Our second insight was how tough it was to admit this weakness.

At first people found it difficult to admit to being anything less than completely on top of things at work. Work life is about performance, so people don't like to admit to vulnerability. Where could you go for help and advice? Colleagues? Nope, they were competition – you wouldn't want to show them weakness. Friends and family? No, they didn't understand the complexities of your work-place. Your employer? Are you kidding?

We encountered different countries, different cultures, different professions, but three common threads – the world was changing, work was becoming a place of doubt not a place of certainty and they trusted no-one to help.

Building a brief

If we really wanted to be true to Monster's values and exploit our insights into the workplace, we would have to tap into the real hopes, fears and aspirations lurking under the besuited professional in any organisation, in any country. Jobseekers were the confident individuals who had already decided to move. Our target was the people who wanted better, but lacked courage, energy or inspiration to do anything about it.

When we put this audience together with the genuine help that Monster could offer, we saw the opportunity to transform Monster from a jobs page to a certain sort of careers adviser. Communication needed to be urgent and disruptive, to make people see that we understood how crazy and confusing work life can be but also that we offered a way out. It needed to redefine their expectations of the category.

To resolve people's desire to find an ally, we would put the advice offered by Monster at the heart of the brief. We would demand that communications create 'a passionate advocate for personal potential'. Our brief brought together in rare combination the uncovering of a deep felt human truth – 'work life isn't easy' – and a group of people united by a delivery channel that transcends geography.

Beware of the voices

The creative work featured people dealing with workplace situations. It dramatised the inner debate we all go through when making career decisions. We heard the voices inside peoples' heads, urging them to inappropriate actions, with humorous consequences. Monster was positioned as providing advice that would be better than listening to these voices.

The idea was based in humour – and humour of a sophisticated sort. This tactic was used to give us licence to approach difficult issues, as well as a great way to show insight and understanding. It contradicted the received wisdom in European advertising that humour doesn't travel (apart from Mr Beanesque physical slapstick).

Despite different languages and cultures, it became clear that the absurdities of working life were universal. Research told us that we had differentiated Monster, by creating "a very compelling, addictive brand character...the style, humour and tone is highly distinctive and lodges firmly in their minds." The best executions succeeded in "taking what is otherwise a sensitive situation and exposing it in a way that you can laugh about it/yourself...this can be a very liberating device."[1] The humour showed people that Monster understood and encouraged them to trust the advice offered by the brand.

We created an idea from a strategy that transcended the internet. It was a brand based in distinct values, not the values shared by all internet brands. We had created an idea that went beyond national cultures, as it was rooted in universal insights. We had created an idea that transcended different working cultures, using humour to unite workers everywhere.

Beware of the voices built a business platform that the company could follow as a vision. More people went to the website (a 59% increase in traffic across Europe), and did stuff when they were there – registering their details or sending in their CV, and they continue to return, consummating their brand relationship. A rare combination of a universal truth teamed with a mass delivery channel allowed us to unite audiences across Europe.

In the crazy world of dot coms, we prospered by putting brand building first. Creative awards followed (D&AD, Cannes), but the real prize is a strong and enduring brand.

[1] Source: Flavour research, June 2000

Public service & charity

The APG Creative Planning Awards

Category Sponsor

NABS was invited to sponsor the Public/Charity Sector and was really proud
to do this. We know only too well at NABS how hard it is to strike the right
emotional chord with people who lead busy lives and need reminding of the
more difficult lives that others lead. The work commended by the APG jury
did just that. It was fitting that the the sponsor of this category should be the
charity for the industry that helps bring those messages to people. Contrary
to some opinion, our industry needs a trade charity as much as the other 200
or so that exist in the country. We help 3,000 people a year with emotional,
financial and professional support.

NABS
32 Wigmore Street, London W1U 2RP
Telephone: 020 7299 2888   www.nabs.org.uk

Special Prize Sponsor – Best use of research

Our business is about understanding people and explaining their attitudes
and behaviour in context to give answers to real business and brand-related
items. We help account planners to understand the hearts and minds and
motivations of the consumer and to get insight and understanding from
research.
We are delighted to sponsor this award for the APG because it is about the
best use of research.
We are one of the largest research agencies in the UK and have an
established reputation for working on major multinational studies both
qualitatively and quantitatively in the UK and internationally.

The Research Business International
Holford Mews, Cruikshank Street, London WC1X 9HD
Telephone: 020 7923 6000   www.trbi.co.uk

Special Prize Sponsor – Best Consumer Insight

WARDLE McLEAN

Wardle McLean is proud to continue their association with the APG Awards, which started in our inaugural year. This year we are delighted that Jane Almey of Saatchi & Saatchi won the award for Best Consumer Insight. We have always believed that research can be the guardian of the good idea, as Jane's paper demonstrated. It is reassuring that the APG recognises the role that good research plays in helping to generate or develop consumer insights. Well done!

Wardle McLean Strategic Research Consultancy
Maidstone Buildings Mews, 72-76 Borough High Street, London SE1 1GD
Telephone: 020 7234 9340 www.wardlemclean.co.uk

Special Prize Sponsor – Best Creative Brief and Briefing

RED SPIDER®

The planner's role is to focus and inspire.
Is the brief a clear, logical and focused argument?
Is the proposition, credible, relevant, and distinctive?
How does the briefing bring the argument to life, in order to inspire?
Keep it simple.

Red Spider Ltd
PO Box 33137, London NW3 4FB
Telephone: 020 7432 0060 www.redspider.co.uk

THE POLICE 'COULD YOU?'

"The first rule of boxing is control!"

"It's not about losing it with someone, it's about keeping your composure"

"But if I was called out to a home, where it seems a man had used his fists on a woman..."

"...beaten her up over some domestic row!"

"I don't know if I could keep my composure with the man. I couldn't swear to that"

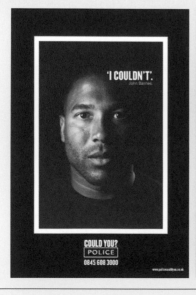

GOLD & TWO SPECIAL AWARDS
M & C Saatchi

Public service & charity
sponsor: NABS
Best use of research
sponsor: The Research Business International
Best creative brief and briefing
sponsor: Red Spider

When respect is due

The Police's exacting requirement for quality rather than quantity of response led planning to redefine the campaign task: to illustrate the level of commitment with the recognition that most people could not do the job. Advertising's role was now to make 999 out of every 1000 people realise they couldn't be a Police Officer, but respect like hell the one who could.

Winner: Richard Storey
Agency: M & C Saatchi
Creative Director: Simon Dicketts
Art Director: Fergus Flemming
Copywriter: Simon Dicketts
Client: Home Office/COI Communications
Product: National Police Recruitment

Introduction
It was a pitch, so we knew exactly what to do.

We'd rush off to groups to 'get to know the customer'. We'd listen to them knocking some of our hypotheses. Then we'd spot one unintentionally perceptive comment. Grabbing that insight, we'd package it up and relay it to the creative team. Then we'd hope like hell.

But in this case we didn't do that. We stopped and looked at the numbers.

A look at the numbers
Our task was to recruit 9,000 Police Officers over three years. But the audience of possible recruits runs to 41 million. That meant we were looking for roughly one person in 4,000.

To put that in perspective, 99.98 % of our advertising effort would effectively be wasted. And even if we'd done groups every night for two years we might perhaps have met one suitable candidate.

So we cancelled our groups.

Instead we started thinking about a different way for the advertising to work.

Finding a different way
The brief asked us to increase the pool of people prepared to consider becoming a Police Officer.

But a look at existing tracking research on the Army told us that already as many as one person in three claimed they would consider a career with the Police. Not only that, more were prepared to consider the Police than any of the other Services.

In other words, the pool of possible applicants didn't need enlarging. It was already too big by over twelve million.

The problem was that not many of them actually did anything about it. Applications to the Police had fallen for the previous seven years.

In other words, there wasn't a lack of people prepared to consider the Police as a career. There was a lack of people considering it enough.

Advertising didn't need to 'sell' the Police, it needed to force people to decide if it was right for them.

Forcing consideration
The Home Office brief repeatedly stressed one thing: quality of recruit. Whilst the imperative was numbers, it was unacceptable for there to be any dilution of quality.

On pushing this point, the response was clear: 'We'd rather not make the numbers than take on a single person who isn't suitable'.

And it was made clear what the wrong sort of person was:

● Anyone who thinks it'll be exciting – catching criminals, fast car chases, forensics work, all that sort of thing.

● Anyone who thinks it's easy – cruising around in a squad car, moving the odd motorist on.

● Anyone who comes into it purely because they're bored with their current job, seeking more variety. That's part of it, but you've got to want to serve the community.

The most useful thing advertising could do therefore would be to filter those who were unsuitable from those who were cut out for the job. In other words, forcing consideration would mean actively putting most people off.

Driving rejection

We therefore wrote a first draft of the brief.

● Task: make 999 out of every 1000 people reject a career with the Police, but one in 1000 apply.

● Proposition: it takes a special kind of person to be a Police Officer.

Knowing this brief wasn't yet tight enough, we sought research to answer two questions:

　– What defines the 'special kind of person'?

　– What stops these people applying to the Police?

Special kind of people

Knowing how inefficient groups with consumers would have been, we figured that the most instructive audience to meet would be serving Police Officers, both recent recruits and old hands.

We began by doing standard interviews, asking them why they chose the Police Service, why they would recommend it and who it suited. But the answers to this line of enquiry were rather obvious and uninspiring. Typically, they would tell us they'd always had their eye on a career with the Police and that it's biggest selling point was its variety – "There aren't many other jobs when every day is different."

We realised we were asking for and uncovering things that would encourage people to apply. Furthermore, they would encourage pretty indiscriminately. After all, who wouldn't be interested in a career with lots of variety, a job for life plus the odd car chase?

Whereas, we'd already worked out that the task for advertising was to put off all but the most committed and most suitable applicants.

So we changed the tack of the interviews. Rather than interview them, we got them to interview us for the job.

Putting ourselves on the spot

The floodgates opened.

The officers instinctively pursued a similar strategy to ours – trying to put the wrong kind of people off, so as to ensure that the right kind of people come forward with the right kind of expectations. They threw everything at us.

- "What is the most important decision you've ever made?"
- "Have you ever touched a dead body?"
- "What's the biggest responsibility you've ever carried?"
- "How do you react to being given tasks you don't want to do?"
- "Have you ever befriended a down and out?"
- "There's a guy high on something with a broken bottle threatening to take on anyone and everyone. Would you step forward to try to disarm him? And if I stepped forward, could I be sure you'd be right behind me?"

And the most telling question:

- "I had to attend at the scene of a cot death the other day. The parents were naturally distraught. The mother kept sobbing, crying out that it was all her fault. As well as consoling the parents, I also had to undress the baby, change its baby-grow for a fresh one. I had to seize the clothing as evidence. I had to take her teddy and bag it up for forensics. Despite the grieving mother I had to make absolutely sure that there was no wrongdoing involved. How well do you think you could have coped with that?"

Faced with this cross-examination, we found ourselves deeply humbled. We had to lie about our answers to keep the interviews going.

Revelation

The innate strengths needed to become a Police Officer were a revelation to us. Here were people who faced profound dilemmas and tests of character almost as a matter of routine.They would describe the most taxing scenarios in the most down-to-earth manner. And, unlike us, these people wanted to take on these kinds of challenges. This was in stark contrast with common perceptions of the Force:

- "Never there when you want them, always there when you don't."
- "All they do is plod around the streets and occasionally nick people for something trivial like a dodgy tax disk."

No wonder Henley Centre research was telling us that respect for the Police had fallen dramatically over the last 20 years. And no wonder also that people felt reluctant to join the Police:

- "Becoming a Police Officer was seen as something that would make you unpopular, rather than respected."
- "Your mates would think you've gone soft in the head."

Respect was key to the whole problem. Police Officers deserved respect that they weren't getting. And potential applicants needed to feel that a decision to join the Police would earn them respect, rather than ridicule.

This realisation crystalised the whole brief.

Respect where it's due

Advertising would not be wasted on the vast majority of people if it forced them to reject the challenge, but increase their respect for Police Officers. The perception of this increased respect would in turn help encourage the right kind of people to apply. And the thing that would generate this respect was the inability of most of us to contemplate doing what Police Officers do.

After all, we respect people who are able to do what we ourselves cannot.

We therefore refined the brief.

Creative brief

● Task: make 999 out of every 1000 people realise they couldn't be a Police Officer, but respect like hell the one who could.

● Thought: not everyone could be a Police Officer.

● Because: most people couldn't interview a grieving mother the morning after a cot death, remain detached while a victim of domestic violence denies the assault or clear a bar full of drunken football fans without incident.

Bringing this alive

With a clear direction to the strategy, the briefing was relatively simple:

● Forget nicking people on double-yellow lines. Think about having to tell someone their son has been killed in a hit and run.

● Forget PC Plod. Think mixture of Samaritan, bomb disposal expert and diplomat.

We impressed on teams that Police Officers do things most of us could barely contemplate.

We gave them a list of examples, we arranged for them to experience this at first hand on the beat and we finished with one throwaway comment: "I know one thing for sure, I certainly couldn't do it."

Bingo

Two days later we had the idea: famous and respected figures admitting they couldn't do what Police Officers do, prompting the question, 'Could You?'

It was one of those ideas you instantly know has cracked it. It was gripping, surprising and had the power to change minds.

The problem now was daring to run it. After all, its negative effects were highly visible, whereas its positives were purely implicit.

Doubts

A secondary objective for the Home Office was to allay public fear of crime. By focussing on dramatic incidents, this idea risked actually raising fear of crime.

When we researched the idea, it was far from universally acclaimed. Many people said it went too far.It would put them off, they said.

Inspiring conviction

We were fortunate however in having a client with the conviction to run the idea. They understood our argument that in research the wrong people would say it was the wrong approach. They understood that willingness to become a Police Officer might actually decline as a result of this approach. They understood that none of this mattered provided the idea provoked respect and provided the right kind of people were prompted to come forward.

And it turns out they were right on all these counts.

When the campaign broke, there was much comment in the marketing and national press about the folly of the 'brave' approach. Willingness to become a Police Officer didn't actually fall, but neither did it increase dramatically.

However, respect did increase. And over 30,000 people rose to the challenge and applied to the Police.

A note on media

We used media to drive the filtering process further. TV and cinema created mass exposure and mass rejection. Even more challenging radio and press work followed up for anyone who still thought they were up to it.

Internet banners linked potential applicants directly to www.policecouldyou. co.uk, which has accounted for over half the positive leads generated.

We have also used media to target ethnic minorities and women without being too 'obvious', using for instance Bollywood cinema, ethnic radio stations and posters in women's changing rooms and 'black' areas.

"Thanks to my dad the NHS now has 10,000 more nurses."

If you voted for change in 1997 - thank you.

Labour
www.labour.org.uk

"I'm responsible for the lowest inflation for over 30 years."

If you voted for change in 1997 - thank you.

Labour
www.labour.org.uk

"I did it. I created new jobs for a million people."

If you voted for change in 1997 - thank you.

Labour
www.labour.org.uk

SILVER

TWBA\London

Public service & charity

sponsor: NABS

The achievement of the people

This paper shows how planning helped create advertising for the Labour Party that successfully communicated positive political achievements in a way that had never been done before. Planning's insight was to suggest that the achievements of a government are the achievements of the people who voted for that government.

Winner: Rob Alexander
Agency: TBWA\London
Creative Director: Trevor Beattie
Art Director: Graham Cappi
Copywriter: Alan Moseley
Client: The Labour Party
Product: The Labour Party

195

"I'd like to say something very unusual for a politician,
    I'd like to say thank you."

Rt Hon Tony Blair MP, 15th November 2000.

Introduction

There are no famous positive political ads in the UK, or to our knowledge elsewhere. All the ads we treasure as great political advertising are negative: *Labour isn't working, Tax Bombshell, Double Whammy* and the infamous *Willie Horton* ad from the US (Presidential election 1988). The challenge in creating a positive political campaign is to stop criticising the opposition.

In November 2000, TBWA\London created advertising for the Labour Party that broke this rule. The *Thank You* campaign is a new form of political advertising. To our knowledge, and the knowledge of world-leading political consultants Stanley B Greenberg and Bob Shrum, this campaign is unique. It communicates a positive achievement message in a way that honours the voters and makes them aware of what they did in 1997 and what their vote could mean in the future. It provides a small link between the democratic process and what happens to people's lives. This is how we did it.

A new way of working

In May 2000 TBWA\London won the Labour pitch. Over the subsequent months we evolved a new system of working that allowed us to cope with the demands of a client whose requirements changed daily, and whose 'market' was subject to enormous, short term shifts that made the normal agency working practices untenable, unhelpful and unworkable.

TBWA created a unique, flexible and collaborative system of working that involved the account team, planning, (Trevor Beattie), the creative department and the client working together to generate solutions in incredibly short periods of time. The key component in the process was the public – TBWA conducted regular focus groups in developing the final product.

This was not a conventional research methodology based on discrete projects, comprising briefing, fieldwork and debriefs. TBWA used focus groups to gauge public opinion, inform our work, test hypotheses, language and creative ideas on an ongoing basis. The successes and failures of the work were briefed back in the following day and further work generated for testing later that week. Thus effective, creatively distinctive solutions were arrived at within the time that many agencies would spend working on a creative brief.

Situation

In September 2000 at the time of the fuel crisis, Labour was behind in the opinion polls for the first time since 1993 (21st–22nd September MORI/*Mail on Sunday*:

Conservative 39%, Labour 35%). Media cynicism was affecting the public mood, with commentators trying to prove a thesis of 'they haven't done anything, they're the same as the last lot: only in it for themselves'.

Less than 12 months from a likely election, this had to be addressed. Strangely speeches, initiatives and normal political activity have limited potential to break through to the wider public, to go beyond the politically involved and interested. Despite the huge amounts of political coverage in the media, most of it is of little use to the parties in terms of communicating their message to the electorate. The media is obsessed with political comment over reporting of message.

Only advertising has the potential to reach a mass audience with a message unmediated by political comment, to reconnect government and electorate.

How to reconnect with the electorate?

In September and October frequent focus groups, in addition to regular quantitative polling, gave us an excellent understanding of the fast changing dynamics in the public's political opinions.

The single most powerful factor in determining overall attitude to the government was achievement. In many cases the Government's achievements were not coming across.

Where there was some recognition of achievement, overall opinion was much more positive.

Regardless of their historic voting behaviour and indeed their opinions on key issues like Europe, it was clear that achievement was the key. The largest single motivator for many people in the 1997 election was change – Britain needed a change from 18 years of Conservative government. Given that desire for change, Labour needed public recognition of tangible achievements to meet that desire. Achievements meant that the Labour government was changing Britain for the better, and that 1997's vote was worthwhile. It was the key to reconnection and shifting perception.

Fortunately the government's record of achievement could stand comparison with any of the last 30 years: one million more people in work, 10,000 more nurses in the NHS, the lowest inflation for 30 years, a nursery place for every four year old and the fourth largest economy in the world.

Unfortunately, when we tried to tell people about these achievements they didn't believe us.

Advertising agencies frequently talk about cynical, informed consumers. We have found that the cynicism over advertising and commercial messages is many orders of magnitude lower than people's cynicism over political claims.

At a fundamental level, most UK consumers know that advertising cannot lie. This gives a base level of trust and comfort with advertising. No such comfort or trust applies to politics. 'Spin doctor', 'lies, damn lies and statistics', 'on message' – all these are part of modern media coverage focussing on process rather than policy, and have in turn entered the language of modern politics. When we hear political claims, our cynicism kicks in and we try our best not to believe a word.

The role for advertising was to reconnect voters with the Labour government by ensuring they recognised that the government had achieved significant change since 1997. To engender the feeling that the government was working for them and the things they cared about. But to do that the advertising had to overcome the public's cynicism over all political claims, a very difficult task.

Finding the solution

The fluid and fast moving nature of the Labour account made the conventional approach of strategic development, and the drafting and redrafting of briefs impossible. Instead the initial briefs were simple and straightforward starters with insights on the task and mindset we were looking to change. The briefs developed with the learnings from research and team discussions.

The initial brief focussed solely on communicating the achievements of the Labour government to the electorate as a whole, particularly those who believed that Labour had done nothing in the last three and a half years. The proposition was 'Labour has changed Britain for the better since 1997'. The supports were the tangible achievements in the key areas of the NHS, employment, the economy and education. This brief produced a raft of concepts and ideas that we tested amongst the public.

Voter cynicism

All the material we tested failed to engage. The cynicism over the claims of political parties was all-consuming. Every angle, every creative idea that attempted to communicate achievement was met with scepticism.

The best efforts of the creative department, the account team, planning and the client were failing to find a way of fighting the cynicism of the electorate. How can you communicate with people who don't believe a word you say?

After two weeks and four nights of groups the pressure was rising. The media was booked and Poster Publicity and our production department had already pushed the delivery deadlines as far as possible. Meanwhile we had no viable campaign to put on the poster sites.

The solution

Three weeks into the project we reached a solution to the problem of cynicism. Reviewing the tapes of the groups, and analysing the responses to the forty plus concepts, planning discovered a common theme to the responses and an insight into the underlying antipathy towards the message. This antipathy was best highlighted by a male respondent's explanation of what irritated him about one particular concept: "They always claim all the credit – it's not them that gives one million people jobs, it's the people who start and run businesses, we give people jobs."

From this analysis planning realised that the brief itself was part of the problem. Attempting to claim achievement for the Government was part of conventional political discourse, and so subject to the cynicism that politicians encounter everywhere in the world, indeed it even reinforced it ('just politicians trying to claim all the credit and exaggerate again').

The solution was to change the rules of the traditional relationship between voter and government.

● Convention: all politicians overclaim their own achievements (however great they are).

● Insight: the achievements of a government are the achievements of the people who voted for it.

This planning insight gave us a new role for advertising, a new way of seeing the target audience and a new message.

It also fitted well within the existing message and values of the client. It states in the Labour Party's Clause IV: "by the strength of our common endeavour we achieve more than we achieve alone" and much of the party's message is about delivering greater civic engagement. This gave a message based upon the people's achievements a resonance that it might not have had coming from a different political party.

The role for advertising was not to reconnect voter and government by communicating what government had done for the voters, but instead by communicating what the voters had achieved by voting Labour.

The target audience was not the passive recipients of government achievement, but vital, active participants in changing Britain for the better.

The new proposition was: "Look what you've achieved since 1997".

This insight and new brief gave the creatives a new way into the problem. As with so much good work, they took the insight and made a leap of their own to make the insight into a truly huge communications idea.

Creative work

Not only was a political party not claiming achievements for itself, it was actually saying 'thank you' to its supporters.

Never in UK political history has a government thanked voters for their vote, nor has it deliberately given someone else the credit.

The *Thank You* campaign comprised a heavyweight nationwide campaign for two weeks from the 15th to the 30th November, large scale door drops and mailshots and a four minute film with Tony Blair, screened in 'the political slot' on Channel 4.

On the 15th November the campaign was launched by Tony Blair in St Albans at a question and answer session with the Channel 4 film shown the same evening. The *Thank You* campaign was picked up by MPs for local activity and in interviews in the media.

The impact of simply saying 'thank you' was enormous. The media comment and volume of coverage of a relatively small question and answer session clearly highlights the importance placed on it by the media. The media coverage only amplified the message and its ultimate impact.

Unlike most political advertising there was no row about the charges being made – after all, we weren't attacking the Tories. The Tories could not attack it because we weren't claiming the achievements for ourselves but giving the credit to the voters.

Results

By the 24th and 25th of November MORI poll for the *Mail on Sunday*, Labour led the Tories by 47% to 34%, a position that was the foundation for their huge victory in June 2001.

The mood of the focus groups became significantly more positive, and when testing concepts and language there was none of the feeling that the moderator was someone from the government facing a hostile electorate, which there had been before the campaign.

Whilst clearly the *Thank You* campaign was not the sole factor in this recovery, it comprised a vital part of the campaign that ultimately lead to a second landmark Labour victory.

The final word comes from our industry journal *Campaign*, not known for its charitable comments:

"It's actually quite refreshing to see something so simple, based on a surprisingly unplundered strategy... I don't think it will get anyone's vote on a jury. I dare say it's far too effective and appropriate for that." (Steve Dunn, *Campaign*, Private View 12 January, 2001)

TV:

Soon he could find out how his rattle feels.

A baby's arm isn't much stronger.

Posters:

By bedtime *she wanted to* shake him *like a rag doll.*

CONSTANT SCREAMING CAN PUSH ANY PARENT TO THE LIMIT. BEFORE YOU CROSS THAT LINE, STOP. FULL STOP. NSPCC

SILVER

Saatchi & Saatchi

Public service & charity

sponsor: NABS

Best Consumer Insight

sponsor: Wardle McLean Strategic Research Consultancy

From paralysis to action

Planning helped move the NSPCC *FULL STOP* campaign to the next important level of public involvement to end child cruelty, over and above making donations. To make the prevention of child cruelty a universal issue – rather than something that happens to other people – planning focused on the reality of being a parent, with the insight that parents of babies are preventing child cruelty daily, in their own homes.

Winner: Jane Almey
Agency: Saatchi & Saatchi
Creative Director: Dave Droga
Art Directors: Brian Connolly, Anthony Nelson
Copywriters: Paul Domenet, Mike Sutherland
Client: NSPCC
Product: *FULL STOP* campaign

The problem

The NSPCC *FULL STOP* campaign was launched in 1999 with our *Can't Look* TV and poster advertising. The role of this advertising was to raise awareness of the issue as the first stage in a campaign to effect cultural change. The *Can't Look* advertising stopped people in their tracks to get their attention. It faced the public with both the issue of child cruelty and their typical reaction to it. Covering their eyes. This launch advertising is the subject of an IPA paper, (IPA 2000).

This APG paper shows how we moved from the *Can't Look* campaign to the next stage where we had to turn the public awareness we had achieved into action. We had to let people know that ending child cruelty was, in part, their responsibility. We had to work out how to mobilise the public into action, without paralysing them with fear.

The focus for this communication was the unthinkable subject of cruelty to babies. The full horror of this is summed up by the fact that the time a person is most likely to die at the hands of another person – murdered – is during the first twelve months of their life.

How could anyone harm a baby?

We knew from the bank of learning that we already had about public attitudes to child cruelty, how difficult it is for people to get their heads around the subject.

Feelings surrounding child cruelty are so uncomfortable that people will subconsciously distance themselves. They tell themselves that cruelty only takes place in lower class or uneducated homes. Or that it only happens in cities – or any other reason that takes the problem away from them. This isn't because they don't care. It's because they can't understand it and they don't know what they could do to stop it.

But the public had to physically do something if *FULL STOP* was to progress. Having shown the public the breadth and nature of the problem of child cruelty we had to move them from abhorrence to action. We had to help people take their hands from their eyes. They had to see the problem and their role in the solution.

Open the door

To move on, we wanted to learn more about public attitudes and experience of being a parent. We were searching for the insight that we could use to open the door. The door that the public was desperately holding shut.

We conducted group discussions with parents with different amounts of experience of parenthood. We talked to first time mums and dads, parents of more than one child and grandparents.

We wanted to know how these people were feeling in the wake of the *Can't Look* advertising? How they felt about being a parent – what were the highs and lows? And how did they feel about the NSPCC?

Can't look – literally

People had been taken to the edge with the *Can't Look* work. The ads had clearly had impact – but people felt impotent and frightened. They felt that something had to be done, but did not know what and still felt that it was the NSPCC's responsibility alone. People believed that their role would be to continue donating money when asked.

This was dramatically confirmed when a 'brand corridor' exercise was conducted with some of the groups. We explored associations with a range of children's charities – Children in Need, Childline and so on. For each room they imagined walking in and looking around and telling us what they saw and what they were feeling. They easily described what they were experiencing.

● In the Childline room: "It's serious, but positive. I can hear phones ringing. This one isn't being answered – so I pick it up."

● In the Children in Need room: "I know it's serious, but it's loud and fun. There are children laughing. There are those great big cheques and Pudsey Bear is in there!"

● But when we reached the NSPCC room the mood was suddenly serious. It was quiet. And then one woman, spoke quietly:"I don't want to go in there. I'll put a fiver under the door... but I can't go in."[1]

This comment epitomised the issue with child cruelty and the NSPCC. People believe that child cruelty is an important issue that deserves their attention. They give their attention by donating money. They also believe that the NSPCC is the most credible organisation to deal with the issue. But at the same time they feel bad that they don't know what they can personally do. They feel distanced and they feel scared.

People were shocked by their own admissions

So the challenge was to create an imperative for them to get personally involved without feeling scared, guilty or overwhelmed. But what about their own experiences of parenting? Could we find the key to unlocking action here?

Parents told us how before the first baby is born the expectations are enormous. You want everything to be perfect. A fairytale. But the reality can be shockingly different.

Nothing can really prepare a first-time parent for this experience. The transition from being an adult who is in relative control of their life, to someone who feels hopeless and sometimes desperate was shocking. The case of the baby-shaking incident with Louise Woodward in Boston came up spontaneously.

People expressed empathy with people who are driven to shaking babies. They didn't condone it, but they understood it. Parents in the group described how they had felt close to this situation themselves and that they had desperately needed some kind of outlet for their emotions. They talked about spending night after night up with a baby crying, at their wit's end not knowing what to do to stop it. And being absolutely exhausted after successive broken nights.

There were times when people had been close to breaking point. Terrible thoughts had come into their minds. One parent said: "I feel ashamed to say it, but there were times when I felt like throwing the baby against the wall. I knew I wouldn't do anything to hurt her – something kicks in to stop you. I just wanted to stop it crying…"[2]

An invisible line

One person's admission that they had at times felt close to losing control led to many more stories. And another shared experience was emerging – the feeling that something kicks in to stop you losing control. The existence of a line was a recurring theme. A line beyond which they don't go. Something stops them and brings them back to reality. They did not know whether it was a chemical reaction – something to do with being the parent of the child. But they knew that they were constantly choosing not to cross the line.

Someone to talk to

No wonder the public push child cruelty away. People don't even feel they can talk about their own experiences with people close to them!

For most, these groups had been the first time that these parents had had a conversation about their experiences. They didn't want to talk to friends or even their own mums because they didn't know that these feelings are normal. They felt they were the only people it happened to and so didn't want to look like a failure as a mum. Their relief on learning that others had had similar experiences was palpable. And although they may not have realised it, or perhaps wanted to admit it, every parent had come close to the edge of cruelty – even if they had never crossed the line.

Feeling connected

Now we had our insight.

It was clear that people find it easier to connect with the difficulties of being a parent than the standard understanding of child cruelty. Parenting felt closer to their experience of life. It helped us to see how we could put the key to change within their grasp and led to a clear and rich creative briefing.

Our communication would reflect key learning from our research:

- That there is a dramatic contrast between the rose-tinted expectations of parenthood and the sometimes painful reality.
- That by showing an understanding of the public's experience of parenting the NSPCC had the opportunity to be closer to the public and to begin a partnership to end cruelty.
- That there is a line, which parents are choosing not to cross – every day. Although the most horrific thoughts may pass through a parent's mind during their most stressed times, they don't carry them out.
- That the sometimes extreme stresses of parenting are kept behind closed doors.

This learning led to our proposition: 'We're all potentially on the edge, but there's a line we can't cross'.

The creative idea

Our creative idea went to the core of people's experience. It focussed on times when parents have been pushed to the edge of reason. Times when they are so frustrated and angry and yet powerless to do anything. Times when they are just about to snap.

The TV ads powerfully and credibly captured 'flash points' experienced by parents. A dad trying to work at home whilst a baby is crying. A mum being driven to distraction in her domestic hell by a child who is continually banging a rattle on a high chair. A dad with baby food running down his hand, as his eyes well up in frustration at his crying baby who won't eat.

We chose not to shock people by showing them cruelty either taking place or having taken place. Instead we showed situations that could lead to cruelty and let the public fill in the rest. As we learned at the launch, this method is far more effective than showing a situation which people can then reject because it doesn't precisely reflect their own experience.

Finally, the end line provides powerful and positive relief: "Before you cross that line stop. *FULL STOP* ".

It also moved the campaign strapline on. It began to make *FULL STOP* more tangible by providing an active and personal call to action. With the scenarios shown it talked directly to the viewer. It made them a participant, not just a viewer.

Different medium – different creative device

We could show the tension mounting on television. But posters had to suggest the tension in a different way. So, we dramatised the contrast between the idyllic view of having a baby and the stark reality.

The posters juxtaposed dreamy images of perfect parenthood with shocking endlines:

'By bedtime she wanted to shake him like a rag doll.

Being a parent can push you to the limit.

Before you cross that line, stop. *FULL STOP* '.

We're on the same side

Until now the public had grouped the NSPCC and cruelty together and then distanced themselves; now we believed we would be able to begin to change the picture to where the public joined *with* the NSPCC against cruelty:

In the end

Planning:

1. Identified powerful themes common to parents – the sometimes almost unbearable stresses of being a new parent and the existence of a line that people are constantly choosing not to cross.

2. This was achieved via a clear and thorough understanding and appreciation of the state of mind of the public in the wake of the *FULL STOP, Can't Look* launch work.

The advertising achieved a higher awareness in tracking (88% of all adults), than the launch advertising – which was already very high, (83%), thus fulfilling the key client objective. There was public understanding of the issue.

Media coverage of the campaign was cathartic – often including admissions that the same types of situations had been experienced. The campaign meant that it was becoming acceptable to admit how close people had come to committing cruelty.

By building on an insight we were able to connect with the target audience and show that cruelty to children is everyone's issue. One that we all have a role in resolving or preventing.

[1] Saatchi & Saatchi research 1999
[2] Ibid

1 Pharmacist

3 Healthcare Assistants

1 Community Children's Nurse

18 months ago Joe was knocked down by a car.

34 people picked him up.

NHS
Careers
Nursing. Join the team
and make a difference.

0845 60 60 655

BRONZE
D'Arcy

Public service & charity
sponsor: NABS

Teamwork makes the difference

This paper shows how planning recognised that the notion of being part of a team sharing the same goal was a new and motivating way to raise the status and desirability of any career in the NHS, and nursing in particular. The planning leap came from recognising that there were parallel motivations to working in the NHS as in advertising: the enjoyment and satisfaction of working together to get an end result of which we are proud.

Winner: Ali Bucknall
Agency: D'Arcy
Creative Director: Nick Hastings
Art Director: Simon Impey
Copywriter: Jon Daniel
Client: Department of Health/COI
Product: NHS Careers: Nurses Recruitment

What is teamwork?

It's about how each member of the team uses his or her individual skills to best effect. It's about trusting in each other's professionalism and judgement to help create the end result. It's about everyone playing a role – no matter how small, in contributing to something of which they can be proud. It's about pulling together. It's about being able to sit back at the end of the day and say – "I had something to do with that" and feel a sense of personal and shared fulfilment.

Which pretty much captures the qualities of teamwork that planning identified as the basis for what has been described as "the most successful piece of advertising the public sector had ever seen ."[1]

A tough act to follow

When you pitch for new business it's sometimes easy to see why it went to pitch. But that wasn't the case for nursing recruitment in August 1999. The previous agency, Saatchi & Saatchi, had won critical acclaim with their *Staring Eyes* TV commercial. The Department of Health's own research[2] had shown that the advertising was particularly good at reminding nurses who had left the NHS of the rewards from nursing, thus encouraging them to want to return. And recruitment figures had indeed been boosted.

A new brief

It would be difficult enough to outdo the previous campaign but the desired outcomes of the client's new brief (and the reason for the pitch) were even more ambitious:

● To recruit 15,000 new nurses over three years.

● To continue to put primary focus in year one on those interested in returning to nursing.

● In addition, to widen the appeal of nursing among younger people (people whom research had suggested had found the call to action in *Staring Eyes* somewhat intimidating).

To make things even more interesting there was another layer of complexity. Not only did we have to continue the recruitment task for nurses and midwives and match previous targets, we had to incorporate this within a new branded identity. The Department of Health needed to address the recruitment problems being experienced by other professions within the NHS, yet which often didn't justify high-profile advertising campaigns. The best way to do this was to find an umbrella brand proposition under which all recruitment activity could hang.

The implication for any campaign we would develop to stimulate nursing recruitment was that it would also need to have an underlying theme that would be relevant to any and every career opportunity within the NHS ranging from porters to scientists. And all this at a time of fiercely negative media coverage surrounding the NHS and falling public confidence in the health service overall.

Understanding the target

The scope of our task was vast. So we started by trying to understand our audiences. We spoke to potential recruits (school leavers, GCSE and A-level students and career switchers), potential returners (those working outside the NHS but still in healthcare, those in non-health related jobs and mothers whose children had now started school), existing staff (nurses, healthcare assistants, managers, secretaries, radiographers, technicians) and last, but not least, the general public (including parents of potential recruits).

We learned three important things that would influence our thinking:

1. The overriding benefit associated with being a nurse or working in the NHS is the sense of satisfaction gained from helping to return someone to health. This was something that was common to all those working for the NHS and an important factor in choosing between the NHS and other employment for those in non-frontline jobs.

2. Yet to talk about this benefit alone was not enough. It wasn't new news and nor did it overcome the imagined downsides of working in the NHS for new recruits. While people retain a sense of pride in the idea of the NHS, the drawings they did to represent working within it (black and white or grey images, large decrepit buildings, overpowering men in business suits, bags of money and weeping nurses) confirmed our worst fears. A career in the NHS is perceived to offer little reward and is something many parents and peers would actively discourage.

3. In addition, existing nurses were dismissive and contemptuous of being labelled 'angels' who have a vocation ("it implies that you'll do it for love and don't need anything else")[3], and angry at their professional status being undermined by perceptions of them being 'skivvies' who merely empty bedpans. Both views were common amongst our target audiences. Both of these views were wrong and needed changing. Above all else, nurses wanted to be recognised as professionals who were good at their highly demanding jobs.

The role for advertising

It seemed to us that the key role for advertising was to create a new reason to join the NHS. A new reason that would build on the crucial motivation and reward of helping people recover, yet create an additional benefit; and crucially a benefit that would re-frame the role and worth of nursing and nurses.

The insight

Initially we considered thoughts derived from the nature of nursing or the other NHS jobs on offer:

- The NHS offers a huge variety of job opportunities. There's more to it than you might have thought.
- It can be challenging. Have you got what it takes?
- We appreciate you. We're nothing without our staff.
- You'll get a lot out of it. A career to be proud of.

But we found something far better. Something that came about not by thinking about the NHS or the job of a nurse, but by thinking about our own jobs. One of the questions we asked ourselves is what does anyone look for in a job over and above the basics of pay, benefits, hours etc.? We sat down and listed the things that motivated us to come to work every day. Aside from the obvious, we all said the same thing. We enjoyed our jobs because we got a kick out of feeling that we'd all been part of the team that had put an ad on the telly or in the paper, and because we enjoyed working alongside a wide range of highly talented, diverse people.

The more we thought about it, the more we felt it was true of many jobs in any walk of life that involved interaction with team members. What's more it sounded rather familiar. It's what nurses had said about their jobs. They said they worked with a wide range of different people, their jobs depended on a lot of interaction and trust with other hospital or care staff.

We took it further and explored the notion of teamwork with our target audiences. We'd found something that was seemingly simple, yet potentially very powerful indeed.

Teamwork was something that made everyone sit up and say "yes – that's what it's all about". Introducing the thought to current nurses unleashed real recognition. For them, working in the NHS is ultimately about working with like-minded people for a common cause – to return people to health. It's a team effort at every level: A&E, theatre, ward, hospital, region, profession, union, etc. Everyone is pulling together to help everyone else do their job.

Crucially teamwork engaged potential recruits too. Teamwork implies that they will learn, get support and have fun. They felt this meant they wouldn't have to shoulder problems alone – that they'd be looked after – something that is particularly important for nervous new recruits and returners who might not have worked for years.

But there was more to it than that. It made other members of the NHS staff feel that they mattered too and highlighted the reward that they'd cited as being so important in choosing to work for the NHS in particular.

The strategic benefits of teamwork

Not only did the notion of teamwork resonate strongly with our target audiences, it appeared to have the power to meet all of our objectives.

1. It implied that the NHS would be a good employer, where the culture of team suggested nurturing, support, modernity and inclusivity.

2. Teamwork suggested nursing specifically would be an interesting, stimulating job in which you meet and work with varied but like-minded people.

3. Very importantly, teamwork also validated any and every role within a hospital and the NHS and gave added status to less well-known professions and nurses alike.

4. Teamwork could challenge misconceptions of nursing by highlighting the need to be able to work within and manage diverse groups of people thus adding professional values to those of caring.

The insight was clear. Teamwork was the new additional value to make nursing and NHS careers more relevant to more people.

The creative work

The creative brief simply stated that each and every member of the NHS team plays a vital role in helping to return someone to health and that nurses were at the heart of the overall team.

The resulting TV and press was simple yet very powerful. It dramatically listed the number of people in the NHS team that helped achieve the end result of recovery. This was summarised by taking the well-liked end line from the previous'campaign ('Make a difference'), and adding our insight of teamwork ('Join the team'). Bingo. Here was an end line and a call to action that encapsulated the idea perfectly.

Our creative development research showed we were on to a winner: the response was extremely positive across all groups with new recruits in particular showing real interest. In addition, there was also interest expressed in other jobs that weren't the specific subject of the advertising.

Tim Mellors summed it up in Campaign's private view[4] : "This spot shows that you don't have to act tough to follow a tough act. Gone is the macho realism (of the Saatchi's campaign), the unflinching detail; instead integrity replaces intensity. Via a cracking intercom we trace a young lad from his hospital admission after a traffic accident all the way back home. The brilliant insight here is to simply reel off a role call of all the trained professionals it requires to put one small boy back on his feet.

Unfortunately I fear this advertising won't be winning as many creative awards but I guarantee it will win a lot of interest from prospective nurses and will end up pinning a nursing medal on many a chest."

The campaign was also adopted by local NHS trusts. Road shows were carried out by the agency to gain the support of the consortia. With this achieved, it was possible to successfully carry the campaign through the line to all points of recruitment, including direct mail, on-line, hospital posters, conference panels, classified ads, careers literature and even business cards .

The campaign has now been extended into other areas of recruitment need, namely radiography, scientists & technicians and pharmacists. It has galvanised local recruitment activity and provided the banner under which all recruitment activity now marches.

What a difference a team makes

And so it has. Whilst results are not the scope of this paper, it's good to know that we're on target. Not for nothing did *The Independent* quote this campaign's success.[5] We exceeded all targets with over 50,000 people calling the NHS Careers hotline during the campaign. Government tracking research[6] also showed significant improvements in attitudes to nursing with 82% of those who had seen the advertising agreeing that there was more to nursing than they'd thought and a 75% increase in finding out more about nursing after the campaign had run.

All in all, not a bad result for us on the advertising side of the fence. Good work that we were proud of made for a happy and fulfilled team of people. Who'd have thought that nurses and ad men would have so much in common?

[1] *The Independent*, 26 July, 2001
[2] DOH Research, 1998
[3] Nurse, D'Arcy research, September,1999
[4] *Campaign*, 17 March, 2000
[5] *The Independent*, 26 July, 2001 (page one)
[6] RSGB pre- and post- tracking research, March/May, 2000

Innovative approaches to marketing communications

The APG Creative Planning Awards

Category Sponsor

MELLOR WATTS INTERNATIONAL

As headhunters, as opposed to practising planners, it was a number of years before we were allowed to become members of the APG. We are proud of our involvement with the Planning Community and our intention is to play an active role as part of that community, doing our best to provide objective advice to agencies and candidates alike.

One of the trends in the marketplace is the continued broadening of the communications message beyond advertising. MWI also deals with many clients and candidates across the broad spectrum of communications. We therefore felt that the award for innovative use of marketing communications was particularly appropriate to us and to the way planning as a discipline is going.

Mellor Watts International
High Holborn House, 52-54 High Holborn, London WC1V 6RL
Telephone: 020 7692 0500   www.mwi-uk.com

Special Prize Sponsor – Best Strategic Insight

Great insights come from a robust understanding of all the issues, looked at critically and creatively. The best planners carefully review all available information and then make the creative leap to insight. As global leaders in understanding how communications build consumer loyalty to brands, we provide some of the information and some of the insights for this process. Ultimately it is down to the planner to synthesise all the insights from every area relevant to brand and advertising strategy and produce the clarity of direction from which great work can flow. Millward Brown are delighted to help the APG showcase the very best examples.

Millward Brown UK Ltd
Olympus Avenue, Tachbrook Park, Warwick CV34 6RJ
Telephone: 01926 452233   www.millwardbrown.com

Special Prize Sponsor – Best Contribution to Media Thinking

Institute of Practitioners in Advertising

The IPA has been a supporter of the APG Awards since the beginning, because we see them as extremely valuable in their own right and complementary to own Effectiveness Awards.

We were delighted to be the sponsor of the award for 'Best Contribution to Media Thinking': we wanted to be associated with this prize to reflect the evolution of the IPA as it responds to the changes in our industry.

IPA membership is no longer just for advertising agencies, and we now represent and serve over forty leading media companies, as well as agencies in many other aspects of marketing communications.

Institute of Practitioners in Advertising
44 Belgrave Square, London SW1X 8QS
Telephone: 020 7235 7020   www.ipa.co.uk

Posters:

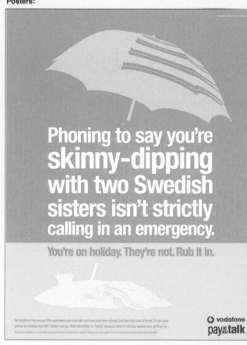

TV: "You're on holiday, they're not. Rub it in."

Innovative approaches to marketing communications

sponsor: Mellor Watts International

Vodafone rubs it in

By digging into the real reasons for communicating on holiday, planning provided a universal and creatively rich insight to drive the campaign for Vodafone's new Prepay roaming service.
The humble postcard provided the insight needed to promote usage –– everyone loves to gloat about their holiday.

Winners: Russell Mitchinson, Dan Izbicki
Agency: WCRS
Creative Director: Leon Jaume
Art Director: David Lang
Copywriter: Martin Gillian
Client: Vodafone (UK)
Product: Pay-as-you-talk roaming

The story

This is the dark tale of holiday behaviour and how the real reason behind the 'innocent postcard' provided the insight for launching Vodafone's new Prepay[1] roaming service. By using high interest groups we were able to uncover the motivations for calling and texting back home whilst on holiday, and formed a campaign around one key truth.

Receiving a holiday text message may never be the same again...

The task

Vodafone was launching a service allowing all its 8.1 million Prepay customers to use their phones abroad. It was the first network to do this[2], allowing their Prepay customers to fully use their phones – inbound and outbound talk and text, just like you can at home.

Fantastic, a genuine USP. The only fly in the ointment was that the brief required us not only to announce this service, but also to encourage usage. Anyone with a contract phone knows the excitement of being able to use their phone from abroad for the first time. Surely an announcement would be sufficient to encourage usage of the service.

Therefore a brief was put into the creative department with the straightforward proposition: 'Stay connected to friends and family while on holiday with Vodafone Pay-as-you-Talk.'

The ads first time round

Some good campaign ideas came back, all based around similar holiday vignettes – 'I've just seen/done something mad/amazing/bizarre, and must tell the folks back home.'

They were very much on brief – not only announcing the service, but clearly prompting usage through depictions of 'reasons to call'.

These ideas were put into research: three qualitative groups – girls and boys (16+), mums and dads and grans and grandpas, reflecting the broad church of Vodafone's Prepay base.

All went well initially. Everyone liked the idea of being able to take their phone abroad, and didn't see why it should be limited to contract customers. Some non-Vodafone customers said they'd switch networks just so they could use the service. And most people took their phone with them anyway for last minute calls from the airport to check they hadn't left the tap running, etc.

We then showed them the ads.

The problem

The younger group loved the ads. They couldn't imagine going on holiday without their phone anyway; "It's like my hand", "I panic without it", and other worryingly dependent remarks.[3]

Mums loved them even more. They couldn't wait to be able to buzz friends back home, tell them about the flight, and find out what's been happening in *East Enders*.

Dads... didn't see the point: one said, "The mobile's not for nattering on anyway", another, "I'd only call back if there's an emergency" and a third, "That's stupid".

It's the familiar problem of how differently men use the phone. Older men don't like to use the phone to chat. It's a business tool, a utility, not a 'socializing device'. Clearly the arrival of this new technology was not itself sufficient to overcome the deeply ingrained attitudes men have to telephone conversations. This was going to be problematic!

As a group, older men were just too large to leave behind. They also acted as 'gate-keepers' to the phone; their lack of approval could lead to a wife cutting short her chat, or the kids keeping the calls brief: "Do you know how much that's costing?", "Can't that wait till we get home?" and so on. We needed a trigger that would encourage their usage as much as the softer target of women and youngsters.

The solution

Obviously some further and deeper understanding was needed in order to encourage older men to use the service. We believed that to do this, we would need to understand the communication needs of our consumers on holiday. Who are they talking to? Where? And more importantly why?

We decided that instead of doing another round of conventional qualitative groups to glean this insight, we would use two high interest groups.

Group one was just about to go away on holiday, whilst group two had just got back. As the holiday experience was top of mind for them, we could use them to really get under the skin of holiday behaviour. We began by asking them general questions about their holiday. Where did you go? Why? What was it like?

We then asked what they took with them. Sure enough, a mobile was seen as part of your essential holiday kit, along with the sun cream and trashy novel.

Then we discussed mobiles and the ability to use them abroad. A familiar response came back, divided along the lines of age and sex. Young people and mums were keen to make full use of it, chatting to and texting their friends and family, just as they did back home. But dads just didn't see the need, and were strongly opposed to it.[4]

225

So we backed up a bit, and returned to general holiday behaviour. We split the respondents into pairs, to ask each other about holidays they'd recently been on. Initially the conversations were fairly cursory, but a clear trend began to emerge. You would either boast about having a fantastic, mind-blowing holiday, or confide that you'd had the holiday from hell. There were no half measures; no-one told of a so-so stay in Bognor, or an average retreat in the Seychelles.

When probed on this, some respondents replied that you spent fifty weeks of the year working, so that you can escape for just two – and these two weeks had to really count. You can't just have an all-right holiday – it's a tale you tell all year round and it must be interesting. Your holiday stories become social currency, to be bartered in pubs and around coffee tables throughout the land.

The odd postcard

We then asked the respondents what they did to communicate this holiday experience (good or bad) whilst abroad. The ritual of postcards was top-of-mind. They appear a strange phenomenon – people are loath to write them, but feel obliged to. However, when pressed, a glimmer appeared. There was something rather enjoyable about this chore – the thought of someone reading your card in rainy Leeds, whilst you were sunning yourself on a beach in Malaga brought a smile to the lips. It was actually worth all the hassle of buying, writing and posting them, just to have the satisfaction of gloating to your friends back home!

And who enjoyed doing this? Everyone, including dads. Even they could see the fun in letting their mates know that the beer was cheaper/weather better/ missus happier now that they're on holiday. So we put it to them – what about using your phone to do this instead of sending postcards?

They all agreed. They could see the beauty of doing it in real time, and saw text messages as virtual postcards; all the satisfaction of sending a postcard, without the bother of having to write and post it.

Hence the holiday gloating insight was born. It was something which united everyone, even the most hard-nosed male users. And it encouraged them to use the roaming service to gloat to those back at home, not just saving it for emergency use. This fundamentally challenges holiday usage patterns, which had previously been the odd call home to check that everything was okay. Now they had a license to gloat, and an obligation – if you weren't gloating, then the holiday couldn't be much good.

The ads second time round

A fresh brief was written with the new proposition: 'Vodafone Prepay customers can now gloat about their holiday whilst abroad.'

Planning provided further creative guidance by encouraging the team to play with the idea of typical usage, challenge the idea that you only use your phone to say you arrived safely, turn emergency use on its head, etc. The resulting press ads featured lines such as:

● 'There is no way of disguising it. Calling to say you arrived safely is a gloat.'
● 'Phoning home to say you're going skinny-dipping with two Swedish sisters is not strictly calling in an emergency.'

Radio consisted of the sound of waves on a beach, or the voice of a sultry Spanish pull, for the 'benefit' of your friends back home.

The two TV executions featured a guy clubbing and a couple kissing, relaying the sound to a mildly hacked off friend back in the UK. All ads culminated in the line: ' You're on holiday. They're not. Rub it in.'

Creative potential

The gloating idea worked well above-the-line. But where else? The below-the-line and media strategy took the gloating insight and used it to create a new habit. By following the journey of a holiday maker, it reinforced the behaviour at every turn – on-line ads on travel sites, in-store promotions in travel agents like STA, editorial in the *Rough Guide*, and inserts in ticket wallets.

When you set off for your hols, there were ads at the airport reminding you to top-up and un-bar your phone, and ads at the destination airport urging you to start gloating. There were even gloating door-hangers in Club 18 to 30 resorts, and gloating postcards in Ibiza club toilets, a source of prime gloating material! The list goes on; from gloating web-sites on *NME.com* to live gloating broadcasts via *Rapture TV*, and a *Virgin Radio* gloating competition.

An ironic youth campaign also sprang from this insight. However to produce a more edgy tone, planning suggested turning the campaign around; look at reactions to gloats versus the gloats themselves. The creative result was fraught friends on the receiving end of gloating messages. Therefore it was a creatively rich insight, producing a truly through-the-line campaign idea.

Did it work?

After only two months of the campaign, a massive 76% of Vodafone Prepay customers (62 million people), knew they could talk and text from abroad.[5] The nearest rival (BTCellnet) only achieved 49% awareness, showing that for Vodafone's customers, we had successfully established Vodafone's number one position in the category.

And even the most mobile-sceptic, low users, the 45 – 60 year olds, wanted to discover more about using their phones abroad, on the strength of this advertising.[6]

Finally

Did planning make a difference to the creative work? By really understanding the holiday mindset we gave an extra dimension to what appeared to be an obvious strategy. Even a rare USP works harder when framed in the context of a consumer insight. And the insight which was uncovered proved universally motivating across the broad Prepay base, encouraging even the most reluctant of users to phone home when abroad. Go on, you know you want to… you're on holiday, they're not. Rub it in.

[1] Prepay is the service which allows you to pay as you talk. Instead of a monthly bill, you buy top-up cards to add credit to your phone, as and when you need it. Unlike Prepay customers, contract customers (monthly bills) have always been able to call from abroad.
[2] BT Cellnet allows its Prepay customers to make calls and receive text messages from abroad, but not the other way round. One2One offers a roaming service to its prepay customers, but it's not like using the phone back at home, you have to dial using a special code and wait up to a minute to be connected.
[3] 2cv qualitative research, 2001
[4] Sadek Wynberg qualitative research, 2001
[5] OMD Snapshots quantitative survey, July 2001
[6] Sadek Wynberg qualitative research, 2001

SILVER & SPECIAL AWARD
Mustoe Merriman Levy

Innovative approaches to marketing communications
sponsor: Mellor Watts International
Best strategic Insight
sponsor: Millward Brown

The thinking man's car

Kia achieved the most successful car marque launch of recent years by telling people to use their cars less. Kia re-entered the over-crowded UK budget car market in 1999 after some years of absence. First, Kia was positioned as not cheap, but responsibly priced. Planning then identified how the theme of responsibility could be extended by encouraging people to think before they use the car at all.

Winner: Garret Cummings
Agency: Mustoe Merriman Levy
Creative Director: John Merriman
Art Director: Mary-Sue Lawrence
Copywriter: Rosie Elston
Client: Kia Cars UK
Product: Cars

A small bit of history

Kia Cars had a troubled start in the UK car market. The marque had been launched in the UK in 1991 with (eventually) three models,[1] featuring as its most popular, the Pride, a basic car aimed at the budget end of the market, in the days when this often meant 'cheap'.

However, with the emerging-markets crisis in 1997, Kia was unable to maintain its position in the UK, and withdrew. In 1999, with the South Korean economy patched up and its companies in a position to recommence exporting all over the world, Kia decided to make another foray selling budget cars in the UK. It then came to MML with a relaunch brief. We now faced 'the Kia Challenge'.

The Kia Challenge

So what would the UK want with another budget car? There's Daewoo, Proton, Daihatsu, Hyundai, Nissan, Suzuki, Skoda… one of the most competitive markets around. And, to cap that, Kia had a media budget of around £1.3 million for the first year, when there's a spend of £600 million for the total car market. How do we get the brand remotely off the ground?

Where do we start?

In the 1930's, each car model was very different from others on the market. However, today, all new cars are pretty similar. There are some small differences, but due to strict regulation and technological advancements, the variation is pretty small. New cars are affordable (on the whole!), reliable, safe, comfortable and embrace technological advances. A differentiating position would have to come from something beyond the product itself.

Kia came to us with some initial thoughts, one of which was that their range was priced similarly across the whole of Europe, unlike other car manufacturers at the time. This was a good start, but it still meant we were talking about cars being cheap. How do we move on?

Our budget meant we had to find an angle that was so powerful that we'd get the cut-through we needed. So, instead of group discussions, we turned to the source of all things topical: newspapers. From their pages, the message was clear. One of the key public concerns was about 'rip off Britain', of which car manufacturers were seen to be key players. Reports abounded in the press of how car makers saw the UK as 'Treasure Island', of how to buy a car from the Continent; tabloid editorials fumed and raged, motoring editors devoted thousands of column inches. The increasing popularity of the internet led to a plethora of dot coms offering cars from Europe at cheaper prices. The consumer's champion, Richard Branson got involved setting up a website to import cars.

Our first insight was simply to take this and turn it on its head: it meant that any car being sold as inexpensively as the Kia range in the UK could be positioned as not cheap but fairly priced across all European markets. It was other manufacturers who were ripping off the consumer.

We produced a series of consumer-champion print ads highlighting the European pricing differential, with headlines like "Fool Britannia? Car manufacturers have been doing it for years", "Worried that car manufacturers are ripping you off? You should be" and "UK car prices are a joke. And it's at your expense".

This strategy would also help us garner positive PR, allowing the tiny advertising spend to be supplemented by free column inches in praise of Kia and their consumer-friendly attitude.

All good things come to an end

This strategy had a fixed time frame. Sooner or later, the bigger car manufacturers were going to feel the heat of consumer ire and reduce their prices. A consumer campaign was gathering momentum; people were holding off buying new cars until prices came down. Car sales fell. And, in time, manufacturers – seemingly – caved in.

In fact, Brussels issued a timely Very Important Directive to say that soon car manufacturers would have to price cars within 12% of each other in every market in Europe. This would be done at pain of the manufacturers having their bananas forcibly straightened, or some other such horrible forfeit.

A price message was a good start but ultimately, cheap still means cheap and our advantage was about to erode. We needed to add some breadth and emotional resonance to the brand. How? The answer came from what was happening in the world of motoring – an even bigger issue than that of pricing.

What's it like out there in the real world?

Again, we looked for a topical issue to give us the breakthrough we needed. Inspiration struck from an unlikely source: a *Panorama* investigation into motoring today. It provided a very clear message from the outside world.

Motoring wasn't the pleasure that it used to be – by any stretch of the imagination. The idea of going for a spin on the open road seemed as quaintly nostalgic as *Brideshead Revisited*.

- Everyone drove everywhere all the time.
- Roads were filled to capacity.
- Everything was geared around the car.
- Lots of families owned two or more.
- All the pleasure was gone.

Instead we had congestion, pollution, contraflows, Swampy, drink (and drug)

driving, road rage, fuel protests, global warming, school runs, joyriding, gridlock.
- Asthma was the fastest growing disease in the UK.
- One billion car journeys made in the UK each year were less than one mile.

Interviews with parents, motoring groups, environmental organisations, local councils and even the odd group discussion revealed the same thing.

And what was most interesting for us was that nearly all car advertising completely ignored the basic realities of driving in Britain today. It was talking a radically different idea of motoring: not even aspiration, but so far removed from reality as to be irrelevant and annoying. It's either some beautiful woman getting into or out of a vehicle, or a car speeding along some empty road in an exotic location: Tuscany, the Californian Desert, Canada. Only a couple of ads, such as the VW ad about car comfort, where a man sits in an endless sea of traffic – and relaxes – got anywhere near motoring reality.

So what possible relevance is this motoring reality to a car company? Aren't they on the wrong side: the side that wants us to buy more cars, and use them more and more often?

How could we use this?

It occurred to us from talking to various interest and pressure groups that anyone running a car company shouldn't be just in the business of selling cars – they're in the business of making motoring more enjoyable again. To do that you need to work in harmony with other forms of transport: cycling, walking, bus, train... Cars are just one tool among many. So how could we go about making motoring enjoyable again?

Breakthrough: 'Response Motoring'

The answer lies in the key phrase that was to become the cornerstone of our strategy for Kia: 'Think before you drive'. If the driving experience in Britain is ever going to be enjoyable again, we are collectively going to have to rethink how we use our cars. This doesn't mean dissuading them from buying a car in the first place, it means encouraging them to use them more responsibly – to see them as one of many transport choices, not the only solution.

Over one billion car journeys per annum are less than a mile. We insist on driving our kids to school – yet childhood obesity is growing. People drive to the gym to take exercise. Doesn't this all seem slightly perverse?

Not using the car all the time would result in increased fitness, less pollution, less congestion, fewer accidents and a reduction in obesity. In other words, more enjoyable.

What's in it for Kia?

There were four very good reasons why promoting responsible motoring was right for Kia.

1. Responsible motoring gave a new company with a minute marketing budget a real way to achieve cut-through by focussing on an issue that people care passionately about.

2. Only a new entrant to the car market, unencumbered by volume and untarnished by a history of motoring irresponsibility could really claim this.

3. Motoring responsibility goes beyond the product. As stated above, there is very little real product differentiation in the car market. Responsible motoring allows Kia a uniquely differentiating position without needing a uniquely differentiated product.

4. It gave people a real, emotional justification to buy what would otherwise be just another budget car.

Initiatives

For such a radical strategy to work, it was clear that it would not be enough just to talk about it in advertising: the whole ethos of the company would have to reflect a real commitment to responsible motoring. It would have to be done with integrity.

What would it mean in practice? How can a car company get a message as seemingly counterintuitive as 'Don't necessarily use your car' across to a cynical public?

We came up with the idea of offering 'Responsible Motoring Initiatives' that came as part of the integral spec of each car purchased, which would show the buyer that we were serious about responsible motoring or "think before you drive" and encourage anyone who bought a Kia to think, and behave, more responsibly. This began with the launch of the seven-seater MPV, the Sedona. Not only was it responsibly priced (within the price range of hard-working families on a budget who needed it most), it came with a mountain bike as part of the spec for use on short journeys. With the mini-MPV, the Carens, Kia offer an RAC risk reduction course.[2] Finally, with the launch of the new family car, the Rio, Kia offer everything you need to set up a Walking Bus[3] in the school of your choice.

Kia also sponsor the British Heart Foundation's 'Walking Your Way to Health' campaign, which encourages people to walk more, in order to help prevent disease. The entire Kia marketing department plus folk from their various agencies took part in the London to Brighton bike ride this year, which was a real success.

The creative

The European pricing strategy was presented in a print campaign with an irreverent, cheeky tone of voice, ready to take a pop at the competition. As the strategy developed, the creative work followed suit, employing a two-pronged strategy: one honing in on the inflated prices of competitors (responsible pricing) and the other promoting the initiatives associated with each model (responsible motoring). All the advertising ended with the strapline: 'Think before you drive'. The most recent TV work launching the new Rio focussed on the Walking Bus, as this was a scheme which had a real chance of impacting the lives of families with young children: the people who'd buy the Rio.

Result

The idea of responsible motoring has not only helped to promote an ethical approach to car use – a unique first for a car manufacturer – it has produced advertising unique to the car market. No more skinny women or Tuscan roads – it's work that acknowledges the reality of driving today, the issues that face the motorist, and actually does something to improve it.

Despite the tiny marketing budget (especially by car market standards), Kia became the fastest growing car marque in the UK in 2000, with sales up 80% on 1999 figures.

We achieved success on the PR front too: Kia was inevitably the hero of all the fuming editorials regarding the European price issue.

Pressure groups like the Environmental Transport Association, Friends of the Earth and also the Department of Transport have been keen to get involved with Kia to promote responsible motoring. We're the only car company featured on the DTLR *Think!* campaign website.

Kia achieved a 0.6% share of the car market in the first year. Comparing spends with Daewoo, Kia spent £1.3m in 1999 to achieve this, whereas it took Daewoo £14.8m in 1995 to achieve just over 1% share – that's over seven times more effective.

[1] Pride, Shuma and Mentor

[2] A scheme designed by the RAC to cut accidents by educating drivers to be more aware of the risks around them.

[3] The school run is the second single biggest cause of congestion. A Walking Bus is a safe way of getting children to school on foot. It's a group of kids walking together in a line that follows a set route to the school every morning, like a bus, picking up passengers at designated 'bus stops'. The bus is 'driven' and 'conducted' by volunteer parents.

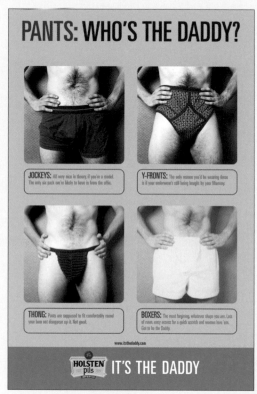

Posters

Beermats

Kebab wrap

TV

BRONZE & SPECIAL AWARD
TBWA, Mediavest

Innovative approaches to marketing communications
sponsor: Mellor Watts International
Best contribution to media thinking
sponsor: IPA

Holsten kick-starts a million conversations

This is a story of how, sometimes, to unlock great creative and distinctive media you just have to stop thinking and start listening. A key insight emerged from observing how men love comparing and having an opinion – the potential for a perfect marriage between an opinionated, outspoken brand and its target consumer that could be exploited jointly by creative and media teams.

Winners: Andy Lear, Jeremy Paul
Agencies: TBWA, Mediavest
Creative Director: Trevor Beattie
Art Director: Brian Campbell
Copywriter: Ben Priest
Client: Holsten UK
Product: Holsten Pils

Introduction

This is the story of a once-great brand, of a brand that needed to feel great again. It's also the story of how following good planning practice doesn't guarantee great work or distinctive media. And how the key to an insight sometimes comes from something as simple as watching people talking.

In the mid-80s, Holsten Pils was the number one bottled lager in the UK. Every second bottle of lager sold in a UK pub was a bottle of Holsten. In 2001, that figure had nose-dived to one in eight.

When it launched it revolutionised pub culture. Until Holsten Pils' arrival the average British male was content with pint after pint of Carling Black Label. Suddenly just by ordering this German brew, by leaning back against the bar and displaying its brown bottle and yellow and green label, he became the discerning man-about-town, the lager connoisseur, the man with style and the cash.

Then things got tough for Holsten Pils. New bottled beers sprang up. Lighter, fresher liquids appealed to younger drinkers. Budweiser stole the crown, becoming the 'badge' to hold on a Friday night.

The market was moving on, so in 1996 Holsten Pils relaunched with younger, more inclusive advertising using the cult comedy of the time, *The Fast Show*. Sales still fell, albeit at a slower rate. Chasing the new 'bottle' audience, 18-20 year olds, clearly wasn't working. They simply didn't like Pils.

Redefining the competition

We spoke to people who were proud about the brand now, and to people who wouldn't rule it out in the future. They said, Pils was a "proper lager", "a lager you grow into", "a lager kids (i.e. 18 year olds) can't handle". It was clear that its strong taste and even stronger aftertaste were defining features that either attracted or repelled. Consequently we redefined Holsten Pils' target audience from 'drinkers of all bottled lagers' to 'drinkers of the tastier ones'.

This allowed us to get a clearer picture of who we could talk to: older individuals who've been around a bit, who are a bit more worldly-wise, drinkers who know their own mind, who can hold their own down the local.

Equally, it told us who we weren't talking to: inexperienced 18 year olds. Getting this clear freed the brand from having to justify itself to people who would never drink it (why would they, when they can have a 'cool' American lager that's far easier to drink?)

Looking inside the brand

So what has Holsten Pils got to be proud about? Well, it was the first bottled lager in the UK, having seen beer fashions come and go (slice of lime in your beer, anyone?). It's a pure beer brewed the German way (with three natural ingredients) in Bremen, not Swindon. And from a brand perspective it has never been afraid to set itself apart, with a history of making a virtue out of being odd or standing out.

For all these reasons the brand was, for a long time, the benchmark against which other beers were measured. We needed to recapture this status. The role for communications reflected this: to re-establish Holsten Pils as the epitome of bottled lager.

We needed to develop a bold, confident brand statement, rather than copy-cat insipid generic beer advertising ("Like me, I'm funny", "Smooth guys drink this stuff", "I come from a cool country", etc.).

The long list of supports gave us confidence that we could be bold. The proposition was equally assertive: 'Holsten Pils: proper lager'.

We briefed it in. And work came back.

Designing the research differently

We researched the work. To avoid 'creative development by jury' and to create a more natural discussion environment we abandoned the focus group format and instead used trios of drinking buddies.

We showed two routes. Firstly, 'The Holsten Truth': Holsten cuts through social niceties and tells it like it is (e.g. a succession of people tell a new mother what they really think of her ugly baby – it's a minger). Secondly, 'Get A Grip On Reality': in a crazy world Holsten helps you keep a grounded perspective, discussing along the way the pointlessness of vegetarian sausages or of plastic flowers, before advising you to always go for the real thing, Holsten Pils.

Although the more relaxed atmosphere led to more talk and the work got a laugh, unfortunately no-one got that animated about it either. And neither felt like the bold, confident brand statement we'd set out to make.

Stop thinking, start listening – the real breakthrough

After witnessing the groups' distinctly average response, and with the prospect of reporting all this back to the creative teams, we put ourselves behind the glass again and noticed something interesting: although the ads themselves weren't causing much of a storm, when asked their favourite ads, the groups lit up: "That Budweiser one, you know, Whassuuuuuuuup...", "No, that one with the German catching the bouncing bombs" and so on. They spoke over each other, arguing about which was the best. They loved having an opinion and amongst friends they weren't afraid to voice it.

Although it wasn't what we'd expected to get out of the research, it turned out to be the insight that unlocked the creative and media approach – men love comparing. Particularly over a beer.

241

Which got us talking. A lot. The best FA Cup Final ever? The funniest sitcom moment ever? The examples came worryingly naturally. Gradually it dawned on us that we were all part of this comparison phenomenon (at last! All those hours playing Top Trumps as a child make sense). Arguing is in men's DNA.

But how could we use this insight to get Holsten Pils talked about again? We knew we had a brand that had never been afraid to voice an opinion and we knew the same was true of our drinkers. We knew we needed to be bold and confident. And we knew we had a history as the benchmark bottled lager. If ever there was a brand that could have the last word in an argument, Holsten Pils was it.

As soon as research had opened our eyes to the insight, we seemed to find examples of it everywhere – Nick Hornby's *High Fidelity* and its endless listmaking, *Loaded's* novelty World Cup series and a rash of Top 10 programmes on telly,

To ensure the 'arguing' notion really was rooted in men's lives we launched a website to ask men what they argued about. It was swamped, we were scared. From pizza toppings to female tennis players to action heroes and *Thunderbirds*, it seemed that whatever men spoke about it was cloaked in comparisons.

The brief went back in, but this time with a stronger creative steer. All the examples of lists and comparisons we'd dredged up formed part of the briefing, supporting a new proposition: 'Holsten Pils, there's no comparison'.

The work

In *Who's The Daddy?* we got the bold brand statement we'd asked for: unapologetic, confident, self-assured. Just what the brand needed to reassert its authority.

Ray Winstone was the perfect choice for brand spokesman: down to earth, straight-talking and confident, he perfectly captured our hopes for the brand. He's been around a while but still commands respect, so when he voices an opinion you listen.

And in each execution, Ray definitely gives us an opinion. A pub philosopher with an underlying air of menace, he debates topics from the best film genre to which is the best flavour of crisps. When it comes to bottled lager though, there's no debate, the Daddy is the original: Holsten Pils.

And if Ray tells you that Pils is The Daddy, it just is. 'Nuff said.

Media gets busy

Both the media and creative agency teams had witnessed the insight. There was as much excitement about it from a media perspective as from a creative one: our £2m was dwarfed by our competitors so a straight head-to-head battle was out of the question. But we also knew that without a great advertising idea to hang them from, non-traditional media are nothing more than gratuitous stunts.

We would make 'comparison' our media property if we could inextricably link

Pils to these existing conversations then every time men had one, they'd inadvertently be reinforcing the Holsten Pils message.

To inextricably link Pils to such conversations meant presenting the Pils message wherever these conversations happened – in the pub, on their way home, on the train, at work, in front of the telly and so on. Thus every medium where these conversations were taking place was appropriate: 'comparing' legitimised the unconventional media we needed to sidestep the big-brand battlegrounds.

True, we still needed TV but it could be focussed on solely seeding the message before then withdrawing from it and swapping to unconventional media in relevant environments, to throw out challenges and get men talking. Recruiting men as our mouthpieces through their conversations became the media strategy: kick-start a million conversations.

What resulted was a range of ambient media that continued to provoke *Who's The Daddy?* discussions wherever blokes got together. We knew what men got up to and where they had to make the day-to-day choices which inevitably lead to comparative conversations: from kebab wraps, talking washroom posters and beermats, to takeaway food lids, special edition Top Trumps cards in bars and an interactive website. Through 'comparing', media leapt from being a passive presenter of messages to actively challenging people and encouraging them to make their opinion heard.

We've got ourselves a big idea

The idea hasn't just been translated into advertising. *Who's The Daddy?* also formed the basis for a PR campaign, a trade announcement capturing the latent respect felt for the brand, a range of promotional ideas, even a multi-pack – 'The Daddy of all packs'.

Has it worked?

1. For the first time in years, Holsten Pils has exceeded ambitious sales targets.
2. The *Who's The Daddy?* line has begun to be adopted in magazines.
3. Have we kick-started a million conversations? Well, we've achieved a total spontaneous advertising awareness figure of 22%, higher than we would have expected with our spend. This is seven per cent higher than the solus TV advertising awareness figure. Its unlikely that our ambient activity alone can account for all that difference: we believe that the increase in ad awareness is the line entering the vernacular.
4. This additional awareness represents an extra half million people knowing the ad line – significant for a brand with only 1.1m drinkers. The cost of buying this extra awareness on TV is three times what we actually spent on unconventional media.

5. The idea has made the brand relevant again. Tracking studies show that after 15 years of decline Pils is now seen to be making a strong comeback, is being recognised by 20% of lager drinkers as the original bottled lager and gaining respect as a result (33% citing it as a high quality lager).

6. Qualitative feedback shows restored pride amongst current Pils drinkers.

7. Perhaps the most telling adoption of the *Who's The Daddy* line comes from Holsten themselves: "The retailers are talking about it – it's getting us more attention than we deserve and we're off their de-list list".

8. The idea has given the company a focus, a rallying cry. Every bit of communication from the company features the line. And its been easy for employees to adopt and use for themselves: "Who's the Daddy of the Finance department?" It's a bonus that the employees have got behind the idea, and begun to play with it in exactly the way we're asking the audience to do. But if the insight is really onto something, then you'd expect them to do so.

P.S. And if you didn't know, most men believe that Thunderbird 2 is The Daddy, apparently.

Special Prize Sponsor – Most Innovative Qualitative Research Design

2cv:
research

2cv:research is proud to support the APG and its awards. We have a natural affinity with planners and help them encourage their clients to make the most innovative use of research possible.

We are committed to innovation in research and are delighted to applaud the APG's continuing efforts in rewarding intelligent and creative thinking in account planning.

The 2cv team is from a broad range of backgrounds and disciplines spanning research (both qual & quant), planning, media and client-side research management. Together we offer an unrivalled multi-disciplinary approach to strategic and creative research.

2cv:intelligently:simple

2cv:research
14 Garrick Street, London WC2E 9SE
Telephone: 020 7655 9900   www.2cv.co.uk

"The ideal car for the woman of today ... 24 pockets and cubby holes to put your make-up and hankies in."

"The ideal car for the man of today ... it's really slinky-looking, so you can fantasise about pulling in it."

SPECIAL AWARD
D'Arcy

Most innovative qualitative research design
sponsor: 2cv Research

When a man might be the answer

Planning's re-interrogation of the brand's existing 'Spirito di Punto' advertising stimulated an innovatively condescending and patronising launch campaign for the new Fiat Punto. Planning helped to establish that 'Spirito' is not just for girls but for all drivers and that, in future, men should exude 'Spirito' too. It then used an innovative approach to develop the potential in men's and women's different responses to the car.

Winner: Daniel Taylor
Agency: D'Arcy
Creative Director: Nick Hastings
Art Director: Dave Godfree
Copywriter: Mark Waldron
Client: Fiat Auto UK
Product: Fiat Punto

Existing baggage
It's the end of the millennium, and Fiat UK was about to launch the replacement to its best ever selling model. A model which accounted for over 60% of the company's total sales, had achieved a remarkable 9% share of the small car market and was the fourth best selling small car in Britain.

In all but name the new Punto was a completely new car, and as proof of Fiat's renaissance it was packed with a host of improvements and technical wizardry. Just as well, since the small car sector had become increasingly competitive with more 'big car quality' being offered as standard. Understandably then, there was a client mandate to reference the new class-leading features in the forthcoming ads.
And speaking of advertising, the old ads are too damned successful. Our existing *Spirito di Punto* campaign was one of the most popular car campaigns around.
According to Sofres' syndicated tracking study, our most recent ad in the campaign, *Girl Watching*, had the second highest recall, and the best branding of any car ad in the previous 12 months.

Furthermore the phrase 'Spirito di Punto' was slipping into the vernacular (we'd picked up footage of *Blind Date* contestants shouting it from Florentine rooftops). Whilst our latest soundtrack "*Music to watch girls by*" had just catapulted a rather fragile and surprised Andy Williams into the top ten.

So how could we retain this hugely successful advertising campaign, but at the same time evolve it to incorporate a new product launch? And how could we include the car's product points within a campaign that was all about empathy and involvement?

A dead end
Demonstrating what on reflection was enthusiastic naivety, we charged at the challenge with relish. It wouldn't be easy, but surely it was pretty straightforward. After all, we had a head start. We had a populist, salient campaign, a unique advertising property that was all about couples, and we just needed to do something distinctive, reference the extras, and hey presto, one car launch coming up. 'New Punto, same Spirito' was our insightful proposition.

Several scripts later and we realised the error of our ways. Focus too much on the couple, and you lost the newness of the car. Champion the features, and it was no longer a *Spirito* script.

Time for counselling
Armed with our efforts to date, plus the existing ads as stimulus, we decided to check up on what people really thought about *Spirito*, the Punto couple, and the value of product features in car ads.

From this initial research of mixed groups among existing and potential Punto owners, two observations we made started to make us think differently:

1. The *Spirito* campaign was mainly associated with the woman in a couple getting one over on the man. Unlike a lot of advertising in this sector, the *Spirito* ads don't demean men. Indeed men enjoy the ads as much as women do. But it is the female perspective on men that prevails and which engages viewers. Certainly in the development of ads to launch the new Punto we had continued to pursue this theme.

2. Men and women had reacted quite differently to the new car's features or extras. Most men had latched onto product information either because of a natural fascination with gadgets, or because it gave them a chance to show off about stuff others may not have heard about. This was especially the case with the 'dual drive button' (or, girlie button). In contrast, unless the benefit to them was obvious, most women had glazed-over when it came to the car's features.

So how did these observations impact on our thinking? As our female planner, Ali Bucknall put it, "for once, the answer just might be a man."

The spark

The planner had started to think that maybe we had been seeing things too much from the female perspective. The research was suggesting that both men and women loved the banter of our ads. So if men enjoyed the ads so much maybe it was time for men to show some *Spirito* too. Maybe we should see *Spirito* less as a female driver thing and more as a Punto driver thing.

This may seem in some ways not to be much of a leap. Hadn't the campaign always really been about both sexes? Well, yes it had. After all the *Spirito di Punto* campaign had never excluded men. Indeed in 1996 when it started, Punto's relatively high male purchase profile had been instrumental in the creation of the idea. It was the reason for having a couple in the first place, for ensuring that a man never looked like a wimp, and for getting male endorsement to whatever film we were about to make.

What we had done, of course, is in recognising that the Punto had a higher than average ratio of female to male owners compared to the total car market (although it was still 60/40 men), we had made the female our hero. This in turn had got us into one way of thinking. Man and woman in car. Man riles woman. Woman, showing a bit of 'spirito', gets her own back.

The thought that was evolving was that given we needed to communicate new product features, and given men and women had such different takes on product features, maybe we should give the man, as well as the woman, a place in the sun. This was a small adjustment to our thinking and it would be wrong to suggest it was the only thing we discussed in moving the brief on. But it was the debate led by the planner on this issue, that gave us a new way forward.

With the discussions we'd had about the potential change of role for our Punto couple ringing in their heads, and armed with observations from research about

251

which product features were potentially fascinating to a man but a turn-off for a woman (and vice-versa), the creative teams went back to work.

Little did we anticipate however just what impact this small adjustment was to have on the advertising solution.

Moving forward

The creative team came back not with as we might have expected, a script featuring a *Spirito* male driver, but with two scripts. One specifically written for the boys, and one for the girls. The two commercials would be almost identical visually, except that one featured a male presenter, the other a female presenter. In both, the presenter speaks directly to camera whilst he/she drives the new Fiat Punto along a sweeping dramatic road.

However, the twist lay in what the presenters said. They presented the new Punto as the ideal car for the opposite sex, and then proceeded to wax lyrical about the new product features in a deliberately offensive and patronising way. The car's features were commended on the basis of the opposite sex's most stereotypical and politically incorrect characteristics, and all done with the straightest of faces. The version in which the man was the presenter was called *Women Eh?*, and likewise the version with the female presenter was titled *Men Eh?*.

Not only were the scripts themselves provocatively tongue-in-cheek-sexist, but it's what the creative team wanted to do with them that made their idea so innovative. They proposed that rather than the commercials running back to back, or even in the same break, we should maximise the initial outrage they would undoubtedly engender by running them in separate breaks so that not all viewers would see both versions immediately. Only across the whole campaign would we achieve a 50:50 rotation.

Resolving conflict

Perhaps not surprisingly client reaction to this idea was mixed.

On the one hand they loved it. It was an unexpected evolution of the *Spirito* campaign, it championed the car's new product features and it appeared to have the required impact for a launch.

On the other hand, there was a real concern that the biggest product launch in the company's history might be somewhat jeopardised by patronising your male target audience with one commercial and then offending your female target with the other.

To reassure the client, and indeed ourselves, we felt we needed to research this idea as thoroughly as possible before we could proceed to production. In order to do this, and explore how the scripts might impact on men and women in a mixed or single sex environment, we devised what we then called 'conflict groups'.

Separate groups of men and women were talked to in order to assess initial reactions to the script that railed against their sex – i.e. men were exposed to *Men Eh?* and the women to *Women Eh?*. Ali Bucknall and Olly Taylor, the two planners who conducted the research, split the groups between them, with Olly taking the female group and Ali taking the men. The idea was to find a way to let the groups express their feelings to the first script in detail and then bring them together for a resolution. When the sexes were brought together we asked them to tell each other what they had heard and how they felt about it. We then played the two narrative tapes again exposing the groups to the other version for the first time. A full group discussion then took place to highlight the pros and cons of the overall approach.

Whilst we had some concerns about the degree of conflict we might have created, in fact the opposite was true. The two groups had the opportunity to express their opinions as strongly as they wished in a single sex environment and were therefore very open to having a vigorous debate when the two groups came together. Men and women relaxed knowing that there were two points of view and acknowledged the truth behind our creative idea – that the differences between men and women are highlighted when it comes to cars, their features and driving.

Living happily ever after

The results of the research gave us and Fiat the confidence not only to make the scripts, but to exploit the opportunity for controversy and exposure even more. As part of the media plan we only ran *Woman Eh?* for the first three days of the campaign in the correct assumption that outraged from Tunbridge Wells would help stir up media interest. And although we bought ABC1 adults with an equal spread of programmes and a 50:50 copy rotation overall, wherever possible we put *Women Eh?* in programmes with a high female audience and vice versa with *Men Eh?*

Sadly, budget cuts meant that the print campaign was cancelled. We were however able to retain the theme of the TV with two finance offer ads that ran separately in the same national papers on consecutive days, and did the same with a tactical ad on hearing that the new Punto had won a four star NCAP Safety Award

Sales of the new Fiat Punto grew rapidly (+ 36% year on year), and the *Spirito* campaign remains one of the strongest in the car market today.

Planner as a back seat driver

Planning often has the role of spotting the opportunity for a small shift in gear or giving an existing campaign a gentle nudge in a slightly different direction. The Punto relaunch campaign is an example of this. It's also an example of where planning doesn't claim to have a Eureka moment, but in the more organic process of discussion with creative teams and other agency people influences an outcome.

In this case planning's gentle probing and interaction resulted in a genuinely innovative relaunch campaign, where two commercials were created to deliberately argue with each other, to cause a bit of controversy and create the maximum impact for our client's new product.